Based on the Terry Lectures
delivered at Yale University

BECOMING

Basic Considerations

for a Psychology of Personality

BECOMING

Basic Considerations

for a Psychology of Personality

BY GORDON W. ALLPORT

New Haven & London
Yale University Press

To Pitirim A. Sorokin

Preface

THE TERRY LECTURER is given the assignment of assimilating and interpreting his discipline as it relates to human welfare and to religion broadly conceived. In the case of psychology the assignment is peculiarly difficult, for the reason that there is no single discipline of psychology. Unlike mathematics, physics, or biology, it is not a unified science, but rather a collection of facts and opinions whose relevance to human welfare and religion depends upon the particular opinions and facts one selects for consideration. Yet despite its diffuseness the psychological mode of thinking is distinctive and is at the present time astonishingly popular.

Each new simplification in psychology tends to be hailed as a triumph of analysis. In recent times either the whole of our mental life or large portions thereof have been "accounted for" by the operation of the reflex arc, by conditioning, by reinforcement; or have been viewed as an associational fusion of sensations, images and affections; or as a dynamic interplay of id, ego, superego; or in terms of some other appealing but skeleton formula. While it is surely the task of science to bring order among facts without needless proliferation of concepts, yet oversimplification brings discredit upon science, and in psychology may succeed only in caricaturing human nature.

Personality is far too complex a thing to be trussed up in a conceptual straight jacket. Starting with this conviction the present essay argues for conceptual open-mindedness and for a reasoned eclecticism. It also attempts to lay certain groundwork that is needed before an adequate psychology of personality can develop.

I am grateful to the Terry Lecture Foundation for an opportunity to present this material at Yale University in the month of March, 1954. For special courtesies in connection with the series, I should like to thank Professor Leonard Doob, Dean Edmund Sinnott, Mr. Eugene Davidson, and Mr. Reuben Holden. Valuable criticism came from my wife, Ada L. Allport, and from my friend Peter A. Bertocci, Bowne Professor of Philosophy at Boston University. At various points these lectures touch on thorny philosophical issues. Though he could not in good conscience approve my handling of all these issues, Professor Bertocci has given me extraordinarily constructive help. For many forms of assistance in preparing these lectures, I am also deeply indebted to Mrs. Eleanor D. Sprague.

Through many years my friend and colleague Pitirim A. Sorokin has battled valiantly to enlarge the perspective of modern social science. In dedicating these pages to him I hope to express some of the admiration I feel for his scholarship and moral courage.

Gordon W. Allport

Contents

No one who attempts to depict the spirit of the age in which we live can possibly overlook the importance of psychological science in the culture of today. It is gradually assuming a commanding influence upon the thought forms of Western man.

Whether we approve the trend or not we see the evidence on all sides. The common man now talks in the language of Freud and reads an ever mounting output of books and periodicals in popular psychology. If he can afford to do so he may have his private psychiatrist; if not, he may be a client of some mental hygiene clinic, of some guidance center, or of a social agency where a psychiatric point of view prevails. In the modern guises of "human relations" or "group dynamics" psychology is penetrating into industry, community organization, and making its appearance even in the field of international relations. Educational practices show its effect, with teachers and administrators conversing in the idiom of Dewey, Thorndike, Rogers, or psychoanalysis. Mass media, and even the arts of biography, fiction, drama and literary criticism borrow themes and techniques from psychology. Adjacent disciplines—especially anthropology, sociology, and political science—often seek their causal laws in the underlying "basic" science of human nature. Even philosophy, the parent of all disciplines, and theology, the "queen science," are to some extent rewriting their principles to accord with the psychological pattern of the time.

In our schools and colleges the demand for training in psychology has reached unprecedented proportions. In the year 1951–52 a total of 2,328 earned doctoral degrees were conferred in the humanities and social sciences in America. Of the 16 fields concerned, psychology was by far the most popular with 450 doctoral degrees, or over 23 per cent of the total number. History, the second most popular field, fell considerably behind with 317 degrees, or 17 per cent of the total. Then came English with 12 per cent, and economics with 10 per cent. Philosophy had a mere 4 per cent of the total.[1] Thus among disciplines dealing with the nature of man psychology, for good or ill, is the fashion.

§ 1. The Case for and against Psychology

MANY critics look askance at the trend. To some of them psychology seems like an illiterate upstart, given to repeating what literature and philosophy have always said, only saying it less artfully and less profoundly. Lord Dunsany once remarked that psychologists, like road-menders, go down only two inches; whereas poets, like miners, go down a mile. Humanists, even while they show its influence, often deplore what they call the arrogance, the superficiality, and the imperialistic character of modern "behavioral science." Specifically they decry the mechanistic assumptions and brittle experimental methods that are the basis of much modern psychology. After examining the present-day science of man one critic, Joseph Wood Krutch, complains that "we have been deluded by the fact that the methods employed for the study of man have been for the most part those originally devised

1. Federal Security Agency, Office of Education, Circular No. 360, "Earned Degrees Conferred by Higher Educational Institutions, 1951–52."

for the study of machines or the study of rats, and are capable, therefore, of detecting and measuring only those cha1acteristics which the three do have in common." [2] Krutch argues for the insights of Hamlet and against the insights of Pavlov.

Neighboring social sciences likewise show alarm. In particular, historians frequently seem to feel threatened by an upstart rival that claims greater precision in interpreting lives and events. At the same time not a few historians employ the rubrics and methods of psychology. Sociologists and anthropologists, unless they capitulate altogether, as some do, frequently take up cudgels against the reduction of their science to psychologism. Some years ago the American Political Science Association appointed a special committee to assess the value of psychology for the science of politics. Its verdict, though not entirely unfriendly, was guarded. Political science, it concluded, should view the contributions of the new psychology *con amore ma non troppo*.[3]

To these and other critics psychological partisans have a ready reply. It is the scientific temper, they argue, that has brought mankind by successive stages from the Stone Age of husbandry to the modern age of electronics and nuclear fission. Why should not the same temper of mind, applied to man's own nature, lead us out of the Stone Age of human relationships in which we are still enmeshed? The more enthusiastic partisans may add: We already know enough about human nature to improve it vastly

2. J. W. Krutch, *The Measure of Man* (New York, Bobbs-Merrill, 1954), p. 32.

3. C. E. Merriam, "The Significance of Psychology for the Study of Politics," *American Political Science Review, 18* (1924), 469.

in a single generation, and enough to reduce tensions among individuals, within groups, and between nations, if only our knowledge were applied by those who are in a position to use it.

It is true, as most partisans willingly admit, that psychology is not a normative discipline. Up to now only literature, art, philosophy, and religion have given us glimpses of what a mature human society should be. Yet, they argue, these models must be lacking in some particulars, else mankind would not have become so badly mired in anxiety and frustration. Perhaps the models and creeds stand in need of modern restatement or at least of dynamic implementation before they can be made effective in an age of atomic energy and totalitarian peril. Psychology is our chief hope for clarifying man's aims and for discovering the means for achieving them.

The debate could be prolonged, extending freely the case for, and the case against, the psychological revolution that is—whether we approve it or not—now taking place. But it would serve no good purpose so long as the issue is thus coarsely drawn. It is misleading to condemn psychology as a whole, or to exalt it; for psychology is not a unitary thing. Unlike mathematics, physics, or biology, it is not a cumulative science but rather an assortment of facts, presuppositions, and theories, whose relevance to human welfare depends upon the particular theories, presuppositions, and facts we select for inspection. The critic, unless he wishes to be merely cantankerous, should tell us what *sort* of psychology he is condemning; and the partisan, what sort he is approving.

Except for a common loyalty to their profession, psychologists often seem to agree on little else. Perhaps in a broad sense, all may be said to be committed to the use of the scientific method—though there is dispute as to the legitimate outer boundaries of this method. Regarding the proper subject matter for study there is less agreement. Some definitions of psychology put the stress on *experience,* some on *behavior,* others on *psychophysical relations,* some on *conscious mental processes,* some on the *unconscious,* others on *human nature,* a few on *"the totality of man's psychic existence."*

Since in this essay our interest centers in the growth and development of personality, we shall consider chiefly those psychological doctrines that advance our understanding of the human person, though we shall also have occasion to criticize doctrines that retard understanding. Not every brand—indeed no single brand—of modern psychology is wholly adequate to the problem of man's individuality and growth. Yet it is to psychology, and to psychology alone, that the assignment falls—the assignment of accounting for the organization and growth of the individual person with all his outreachings, downward, upward, inward, outward. If present-day psychology is not fully equal to the task then we should improve the science until it is.

Other sciences have different concerns. For example, sociology by contrast views the person as a part of his family, his group, his nation; the anthropologist views him as part of a culture. The theologian focuses attention on his spiritual aspects and relates them to a presumed divine scheme. In a similar way political science, economics, and other so-called "behavior sciences" ablate an aspect of personal conduct from the integral nexus of personality, and relate this aspect to some outer frame of

5

reference. They provide us with a picture of the political man in relation to a political system, or of the economic man in relation to the economic system, but not of the whole man in relation to his own individual system. The biologist, physiologist and biochemist retreat still further, deliberately avoiding the phenomena both of total organization and of consciousness, and thus reduce the person to something less than a complete system for study. To the psychologist alone falls the problem of the complete psychophysical organization. In principle he cannot be satisfied with segments of persons related to outer coordinates. He must consider the system as a whole, and show how part systems are related to one another.

But his ways of viewing the system as a whole are distressingly diverse. Is it governed from without, or governed from within? Is it merely reactive or is it active, mechanically determined or in some degree spontaneous? (It is on this issue, above all others, that we find psychologists dividing.) Some current theories of personality are Aristotelian in their acceptance of entelechy; some—a growing number at the moment—seek an answer, as did Descartes, in the phenomenology of cognition. Many (the Freudians among them) are disciples of Schopenhauer in accepting the primacy of a blindly acting will. Others, the neo-Thomists, see the human person as both a striving and rational being approaching toward, or departing from, an ideal of perfection according to his exercise of freedom.[4] Psychologists gravitate toward one or another

4. Cf. Magda B. Arnold and J. A. Gasson, S.J., *The Human Person: An Approach to an Integral Theory of Personality*, New York, Ronald Press, 1954.

6

philosophical assumption regarding the nature of man, often without being fully aware that they do so.

We cannot here attempt to depict all of the current psychological schools of thought with their diverse philosophical assumptions. It will be helpful for our purposes, however, to have in mind two broadly contrasting approaches to the problem of man's becoming. Virtually all modern psychological theories seem oriented toward one of two polar conceptions, which, at the risk of some historical oversimplification, I shall call the Lockean and the Leibnitzian traditions respectively. It is not the total philosophy of Locke or of Leibnitz that is here in question. Rather it is their views on one aspect of man's mind —its essentially passive nature (Locke) or its active nature (Leibnitz)—that I wish to contrast. The same polarity, as I say, is found in current theories of growth and change in human personality.

§ 2. *The Lockean Tradition*

JOHN LOCKE, we all recall, assumed the mind of the individual to be a *tabula rasa* at birth. And the intellect itself was a passive thing acquiring content and structure only through the impact of sensation and the crisscross of associations, much as a pan of sweet dough acquires tracings through the impress of a cookie cutter. Locke insisted that there can be nothing in the intellect that was not first in the senses (*nihil est in intellectu quod non fuerit in sensu*).

7

To this formula Leibnitz added a challenging supplement: nothing—save only the intellect itself (*excipe: nisi ipse intellectus*). To Leibnitz the intellect was perpetually active in its own right, addicted to rational problem solving, and bent on manipulating sensory data according to its own inherent nature. For Locke the organism was reactive when stimulated; for Leibnitz it was self-propelled. Perhaps it is because Locke was an Englishman that his way of thinking, elaborated by Hume and a host of like-minded successors, became so firmly established in the psychology of Britain and America; whereas Leibnitz' view, developed by Kant, has, generally speaking, prevailed in German psychology and elsewhere on the Continent.

We cannot, of course, expect the entire history of psychology to be neatly ordered to this simple, basic dichotomy. Any given system of thought may well show traces of both historical models, and to a degree both are correct and useful. Yet it will be instructive to pass in brief review the viewpoints in contemporary psychology that are heavily Lockean in their emphasis, and those that are Leibnitzian.

The Lockean point of view, as I have said, has been and is still dominant in Anglo-American psychology. Its representatives are found in associationism of all types, including environmentalism, behaviorism, stimulus-response (familiarly abbreviated as S-R) psychology, and all other stimulus-oriented psychologies, in animal and genetic psychology, in positivism and operationism, in mathematical models—in short, in most of what today is cherished in our laboratories as truly "scientific" psychology. These movements, diverse though they may appear at first sight, have in common with Lockean empiricism certain fundamental presuppositions.

First of all they hold that what is external and visible is more fundamental than what is not. Since mind is by nature a tabula rasa, it is not the organism itself but what happens to the organism from the outside that is important. Even motives, which would seem to be as central and spontaneous as anything within the personality, are regarded as "drives," a mere matter of change in the condition of peripheral tissues, due usually to the excess or deficit stimulation in the body cavities. To account for motives more complex than drives we are told that *drive*-instigated behavior may when conditioned give way to *cue*-instigated behavior. The "cause" remains external to the organism.

Although the principle of conditioning was discovered by Pavlov in Russia, the alacrity with which it was seized upon and developed by American psychologists shows its close kinship with the prevailing Lockean tradition. Learning is regarded as the substitution of one effective stimulus for another or of one response for another. In either event what happens between the stimulus and the response (in what Leibnitz would call the intellect) is regarded as of little or no importance. Even the grudging admission in recent years that so-called "intervening variables" may be needed to render a more adequate account of behavior represents, for the most part, a minimal departure from the S-R model. And we note that the doctrine of conditioning offers a physiological description in place of "organization of ideas." This externalization further helps to account for its popularity.

A further presupposition of Lockean empiricism is that

what is small and molecular (cf. Locke's "simple ideas") is more fundamental than what is large and molar (Locke's "complex ideas"). In the modern day, human personality is regarded as a concatenation of reflexes or of habits. For Hull as for Watson it is a habit-hierarchy. The upper reaches of the hierarchy receive little attention. It is the habit unit itself that preoccupies the attention of most psychologists working in the field of learning, growth, and development.

Preoccupation with molecular units brings with it a strong belief in the equivalence of species. This view says that every basic feature of human nature can be studied without essential loss among lower species. Since man is an animal, why not take animals that are simpler—the rat for instance—as a prototype of the more complicated animal? Species equivalence is widely accepted in contemporary psychology, although the assumption is sometimes stated with caution. Thus Professor Hull, one of our leading American empiricists, wrote: "Humans have the added capacity of speech, symbolic behavior, with the accompanying advantages of the higher mental processes. Whether this introduces any primary behavioral laws remains to be determined." [5] While Professor Hull thus wishes to remain open-minded, his statement clearly argues for a provisional faith in species equivalence.

One final presupposition marks Lockean empiricism, namely, the assumption that what is earlier is more fundamental than what is late in development. The early impress upon the wax of the mind is important. First impressions, to be sure, may later be compounded and criss-

5. C. L. Hull, *A Behavior System* (New Haven, Yale University Press, 1952), p. 4.

10

crossed, but the original simple ideas are still the elements of later mental life. This type of geneticism has taken a firm hold upon American psychology.[6] In keeping with the doctrine of tabula rasa, American geneticism holds that what is important is childhood learning, childhood fixations, childhood conditioning. We shall see later that this point of view creates considerable difficulty for a theory of growth and change in personality.

All of these Lockean presuppositions are congenial to modern positivism. In keeping with the preference for visible externals, positivism (operationism) holds that the devices employed in experimentation or measurement shall be specified in the definitions of every concept. The ideal behind this stringent requirement is to bring psychology into line with physics and mathematics so as to make for a unity of science. Positivism desires to reduce abstract concepts to the data of observation or to the process of observation itself. In spite of reluctant concessions to verbal reporting as an allowable operation under certain circumstances, the sparseness that results from the application of operational criteria discourages the investigation of consciousness as a datum, as well as of personality as a complex structure, for in these domains relatively few concrete operations can be performed, few are repeatable, and few are public.

Precisely here we find the reason why so many psychologists fail to take an interest in the existential richness of human life. Methods, they say, are lacking. Or, more ex-

6. I am not speaking of geneticism in the sense of inherited or constitutional predispositions but in the sense of early learning. It is unfortunate that "geneticism" has these two divergent meanings.

actly stated, the methods available fall short of the stringent requirements laid down by modern positivism. In
their desire to emulate the established sciences psychologists are tempted to tackle only those problems, and to
work on only those organisms, that yield to acceptable
operations. For this reason we find animal psychology and
mathematical psychology highly developed. So dominant
is the positivistic ideal that other fields of psychology
come to be regarded as not quite reputable. Special aversion attaches to problems having to do with complex
motives, high-level integration, with conscience, freedom,
selfhood. As we have said, in large part it is the relative
lack of objective methods of study that accounts for this
aversion. But the explanation lies also in the preference
of positivism for externals rather than internals, for elements rather than patterns, for geneticism, and for a
passive or reactive organism rather than for one that is
spontaneous and active.

§ 3. *The Leibnitzian Tradition*

THE LEIBNITZIAN tradition, by contrast, maintains
that the person is not a collection of acts, nor simply the
locus of acts; the person is the *source* of acts. And activity
itself is not conceived as agitation resulting from pushes
by internal or external stimulation. It is purposive. To
understand what a person is, it is necessary always to refer
to what he may be in the future, for every state of the
person is pointed in the direction of future possibilities.
Aristotle's doctrines of orexis and entelechy anticipated

12

the spirit of Leibnitz, as did the doctrine of intention in St. Thomas Aquinas. Spinoza insisted that *conatus,* the striving toward self-preservation and self-affirmation, is the secret of all becoming. In more recent times Franz Brentano has held that at every moment of time the human mind is both active and pointed, engaged endlessly in judging, comparing, comprehending, loving, desiring, avoiding. To him the model for mind is the active participle. To John Dewey it was the verb, no less the token of an active intellect.

It will help us to comprehend this tradition in its present form if we look first at contemporary cognitive psychology and then at theories of motivation. Kant's view of inherent categories, of the forms of thought, was opposed to the tabula rasa of Locke. Herbart, Brentano, and Wundt (with his theory of creative apperceptive synthesis) continued to reach beyond the mechanics of associationism for an explanation of mental organization. The active intellect was preserved (still on the Continent we note) in the Würzburg doctrines of attitude, set, and tendency. Von Ehrenfels' insistence that cognitive structure maintains a form-quality even when no single element is preserved (as in the transposition of melodies) led to the Gestalt movement, whose work is concerned almost entirely with dynamic principles of cognition. Concepts of *closure, self-distribution, Prägnanz, insight* all call attention to the inherent activity of the intellect that molds, arranges, interprets sensory data in ways not allowed for by elementarist theories derived from Locke and Hume.

While Gestalt psychology is the most influential version of the active intellect to reach America, it is interesting indeed to see what has happened to it in the process

13

of adjusting to Anglo-Saxon empiricism. Americans who have recently embraced so-called "cognitive theory" seldom go so far as to accept the whole array of Gestalt concepts; for the most part they have little use for dynamical self-distribution, Prägnanz, or insight. They prefer a minimum of such autochthonous activity in the intellect (or brain). In place of *intention* they prefer the more passive concept *expectancy*. In place of planning, foresight, or purpose, American cognitive theorists prefer the more static conception of *cognitive maps* or *sets*. But even these diluted versions of the active intellect are strenuously challenged by those American positivists who keep to the tradition of stimulus-response reactivity and associationism. We may view positivism (including not only behaviorism and operationism but also associationism) as the right wing of contemporary American psychology; so-called cognitive theory as the left wing. But cognitive theory as found in America today is not very far to the left. It is still Lockean as compared with a truly active intellect intrinsic to the personal self as envisaged by Leibnitz and his successors.

Briefly then, the present situation in cognitive psychology can be described in four statements. 1. The full-scale phenomenology which presupposes an active thinker and a primary process of relating this thinker to his own states of consciousness—represented in varying degrees by Brentano, Husserl, Scheler, and others—has led to a flourishing school of epistemology, but because of its inherent subjectivity has had little direct influence upon American psychology. 2. The Gestalt school, though indirectly influenced by this philosophical phenomenology, is grounded in the experimental tradition, and has led especially in Europe to a rich store of concepts that presume the existence of an active intellect (e.g., dynamical self-distribution, belongingness, insight, closure). Unlike phenomenology proper, Gestalt theory does not place primary emphasis upon the subject-object relationship, but on varied dynamic processes, each considered in its own right. 3. In American cognitive theory the concepts of Gestalt psychology have been considerably diminished so far as their emphasis upon self-activity (autochthonous process) is concerned, with the substitution of less dynamic concepts such as hypothesis, expectancy, cognitive maps. 4. Many American positivists and associationists repudiate all such conceptions, even the dilute American cognitive theory, and hold that the conceptual frame of stimulus-response theory is adequate, and that the hypothesis of the "empty organism" is preferable to the assumption of an organism furnished with a self-active intellect.

But no theory of cognition, however dynamic, would give us the required foundation for a full-bodied psychology of personality. We need also a doctrine of motivation to explain the facilitating, inhibiting, selecting, and vivifying of our cognitive and behavioral systems. While no modern psychologist would doubt this fact, there is as wide a difference among views of motivation as among views of cognition. We have already noted the rigorous parsimony that guides the drive and conditioning theories so popular in American laboratories today.

By contrast there are those who, more in keeping with the tradition of Leibnitz' self-active monads, envisage motivation in a wholly different way. Some believe that instincts—more broadly conceived than drives—are cen-

15

tral to all behavior, to all thought, to all adjustment, to all living. Some advocates of instinct are vague in respect to their taxonomy, as is Freud; some are remarkably specific, as is McDougall. Yet any doctrine of plural instincts tends to occupy a halfway station between the poles of activity and reactivity. It is true that the urge quality of the instinct is self-contained within the organism (not resident in the stimulus instigator, as positivists would like to believe), but instincts are after all multiple "forces" to which the individual is subject. He is pushed, pulled, and mauled by their energies. He himself is devoid of energy or purpose except as the instincts themselves provide them.

Beyond the theory of plural instincts we find certain modern writers whose central conceptions parallel Spinoza's doctrine of conatus. One thinks in this connection of Goldstein's emphasis upon self-actualization, of the writings of Angyal, Cantril, Lecky, Revers, Sinnott, and others who in common postulate one basic motive in life —the maintaining, actualizing, and enhancing of the capacities of the experiencing organism.[7]

With this line of thought we reach the polar opposite to Locke's portrait of mind as a passive receptacle receiving

7. Cf. K. Goldstein, *Human Nature in the Light of Psychopathology*, Cambridge, Harvard University Press, 1940; A. Angyal, *Foundations for a Science of Personality*, New York, Commonwealth Foundation, 1941; H. Cantril, *The "Why" of Man's Experience*, New York, Macmillan, 1950; P. Lecky, *Self-consistency: A Theory of Personality*, New York, Island Press, 1945; W. J. Revers, *Charakterprägung und Gewissensbildung*, Nürnberg, Sebaldus Verlag, 1951; E. W. Sinnott, "The Biology of Purpose," *American Journal of Orthopsychiatry*, 22 (1952), 457–68.

external engravings, and the opposite to Hume's conception of the self as a bundle of sensations.

§ 4. The Goal of Psychology

THE GOAL of psychology is to reduce discord among our philosophies of man, and to establish a scale of probable truth, so that we may feel increasingly certain that one interpretation is truer than another. The goal is as yet unattained; as our discussion suggests, it probably lies far in the future.

Since psychology is new at its job we must expect a lively spirit of controversy to prevail. Fortunately, creative controversy is possible in our free society. It is probably a good thing to have Lockeans and Leibnitzians, positivists and personalists, Freudians and neo-Freudians, objectivists and phenomenologists; those who favor mathematical models, animal models, mechanical models, psychiatric models—or no models. They cannot all be correct in all particulars, but it is essential that they have freedom to work in their own ways.

Our censure should be reserved for those who would close all doors but one. The surest way to lose truth is to pretend that one already wholly possesses it. For narrow systems, dogmatically held, tend to trivialize the mentality of the investigator and of his students. Sad to relate, we have examples of such trivialization in psychology today. One degrading form is the restrictive mentality that certain positivists would impose. Theory, they tell

17

us, is senseless, at least theory that deals with the inner workings of man's nature. They advise us to derive our concepts solely from our methods of study, never from the assumed functioning of human life, even though concepts derived from method can tell us only about method and nothing about the nature of man's being or becoming. But operationism is not the only agent of intolerance. Some devotees of Freudianism, phenomenology, Thomism, and other preferred schools of thought also close all doors but their own. Dogmatism makes for scientific anemia.

It is especially in relation to the formation and development of human *personality* that we need to open doors. For it is precisely here that our ignorance and uncertainty are greatest. Our methods, however well suited to the study of sensory processes, animal research, and pathology, are not fully adequate; and interpretations arising from the exclusive use of these methods are stultifying. Some theories of becoming are based largely upon the behavior of sick and anxious people or upon the antics of captive and desperate rats. Fewer theories have derived from the study of healthy human beings, those who strive not so much to preserve life as to make it worth living. Thus we find today many studies of criminals, few of law-abiders; many of fear, few of courage; more on hostility than on affiliation; much on the blindness in man, little on his vision; much on his past, little on his outreaching into the future.

The major task of psychology today is to enlarge its horizons without sacrificing its gains. No one wants adequacy of outlook if the resulting system remains a tissue

18

of unverifiable assertions; but neither can one derive satisfaction from mere accuracy if its productions are largely irrelevant to root problems.

The course we shall pursue is to identify the major issues that confront a psychology of becoming, and offer provisional solutions based on preliminary evidence. We can only trust that future research conducted with an open mind will strengthen or amend our provisional solutions with the aid of new evidence of requisite accuracy.

§ 5. The Dilemma of Uniqueness

PERSONALITY is less a finished product than a transitive process. While it has some stable features, it is at the same time continually undergoing change. It is this course of change, of becoming, of individuation that is now our special concern.

The first fact that strikes us is the uniqueness of both the process and the product. Each person is an idiom unto himself, an apparent violation of the syntax of the species. An idiom develops in its own peculiar context, and this context must be understood in order to comprehend the idiom. Yet at the same time, idioms are not entirely lawless and arbitrary; indeed they can be known for what they are only by comparing them with the syntax of the species.

Now the scientific training of the psychologist leads him to look for universal processes common to the species, and to neglect the idiomatic pattern of becoming. While he may *say* that his subject matter is human personality, his habits lead him to study mind-in-general rather than mind-in-particular.

It is not that the psychologist is uninterested in John, the person. It is merely that his habits of thought lead him to ablate from John's nature some single segment for study. The surgery is accomplished by impressing upon John certain universal cutting instruments. One incision has to do, shall we say, with the "need for achievement," another with the "intelligence quotient." These incisions are not viewed as intersecting one another in John but rather as intersecting corresponding properties in other persons. The result is that we usually view John's personality as a diagram drawn in a set of external co-ordinates, having no interrelations, no duration in time, no motion, no life, no variability, no uniqueness. What is peculiarly Johnian our methods of analysis do not tell.

It is true that the branch of psychology called "clinical" hopes somehow to bring about a coincidence of John with the properties abstracted from him. It endeavors to reclaim him from the sea of statistical averages. But for two reasons it runs into trouble. In the first place, as we have said, the universal dimensions employed in diagnosing John may be irrelevant to his personality. Perhaps he has no "need for achievement" but only a peculiar and unique need for exhibitionistic domination. The dimension employed seriously misses the precise coloring of his motivation. In the second place, we have few tools as yet to determine the mutual interrelations of dimensions. Thus we discover only that John stands at the tenth percentile on "need achievement," at the fiftieth in ability at "spatial manipulation," at the eighty-first percentile on "common responses" to the Rorschach test. Such bits of information comprise most clinical reports. Seldom do these bits of information intersect one another. We are still in the dark concerning the nexus of John's life. A large share of our trouble lies in the fact that the elements we employ in our analyses are not true parts of the original whole.

It is not helpful, I think, to reply that science, by its very nature, is impotent in the face of the idiomatic process of becoming. If there is to be a science of personality at all it should do better than it has in the past with the feature of personality that is most outstanding—its manifest uniqueness of organization.

Nor is it helpful to take refuge in the example of other sciences. We are told that every stone in the field is unique, every old shoe in the closet, every bar of iron, but that this ubiquitous individuality does not affect the operations or the progress of science. The geologist, the physicist, the cobbler proceed to apply universal laws, and find the accident of uniqueness irrelevant to their work. The analogy is unconvincing. Stones, old shoes, bars of iron are purely reactive; they will not move unless they are manipulated. They are incapable of becoming. How is it then with uniqueness in the realm of biology where in addition to reactivity each plant manifests the capacities for self-repair, self-regulation, adaptation? One leaf on the tree is large, another small, one deformed, another healthy. Yet all obey the sure laws of metabolism and cell structure. It is only in our aesthetic moments that we are interested in the precise shape, size, form, or individuality of a given leaf, plant, or animal.

But here too the analogy is weak. Unlike plants and lower animals, man is not merely a creature of cell structure, tropism, and instinct; he does not live his life by repeating, with trivial variation, the pattern of his species. Nature's heavy investment in individuality stands forth chiefly in *homo sapiens*. While we may recognize individual differences among dogs or varying strains of temperament among rats, still their lives in all essential particulars are regulated by their membership in a species. Man alone has the capacity to vary his biological needs extensively and to add to them countless psychogenic needs reflecting in part his culture (no other creature has a culture), and in part his own style of life (no other creature worries about his life-style).

Hence the individuality of man extends infinitely beyond the puny individuality of plants and animals, who are primarily or exclusively creatures of tropism or instinct. Immense horizons for individuality open when billions of cortical cells are added to the meager neural equipment of lower species. Man talks, laughs, feels bored, develops a culture, prays, has a foreknowledge of death, studies theology, and strives for the improvement of his own personality. The infinitude of resulting patterns is plainly not found in creatures of instinct. For this reason we should exercise great caution when we extrapolate the assumptions, methods, and concepts of natural and biological science to our subject matter. In particular we should refuse to carry over the indifference of other sciences to the problem of individuality.

Emulation of an older science never creates a newer science. It is only unquenchable curiosity about some persistent phenomenon of nature that does so. Individuality,

I argue, is a legitimate object of curiosity, especially at the human level, for it is here that we are overwhelmed by this particular natural phenomenon. I venture the opinion that all of the animals in the world are psychologically less distinct from one another than one man is from other men.

There are, of course, many areas of psychology where individuality is of no concern. What is wanted is knowledge about averages, about the generalized human mind, or about types of people. But when we are interested in guiding, or predicting John's behavior, or in understanding the Johnian quality of John, we need to transcend the limitations of a psychology of species, and develop a more adequate psychology of personal growth.

The outlines of the needed psychology of becoming can be discovered by looking within ourselves; for it is knowledge of our own uniqueness that supplies the first, and probably the best, hints for acquiring orderly knowledge of others. True, we should guard against the fallacy of projection: of assuming that other people have states of mind, interests, and values precisely like our own. Yet it is by reflecting upon the factors that seem vital in our own experience of becoming that we identify the issues that are important. When we ask ourselves about our own course of growth such problems as the following come to mind: the nature of our inborn dispositions, the impress of culture and environment upon us, our emerging self-consciousness, our conscience, our gradually evolving style of expression, our experiences of choice and freedom, our handling of conflicts and anxieties, and finally the formation of our maturer values, interests, and aims. While many of these topics receive occasional treatment in modern psychology, they are seldom surveyed in relation to one another as we shall now attempt to do.

§ 6. Disposition

INBORN dispositions, the raw material for the development of personality, comprise at least three sets of factors. First are those tendencies common to the species that make for survival—an array of reflexes, drives, and homeostatic processes. Anything that can properly be called instinctive falls into this class. At the present time we seem to be on the threshold of marked advances in knowledge of the nature of instinct. From the work of Lashley, Tinbergen, Spitz and Wolf, and others we know that complex social behavior evolves in part from simple responses that are activated by patterned stimuli. As yet we have no idea how many of these "innate releaser mechanisms" there may be. A single example is the social smile, studied by Spitz and Wolf.[8] A period of maturation seems to occur, lasting roughly from the age of three to six months when the infant, to the delight of all, engages in the social smile. Smiles prior to that age are probably due to digestive activity. The normal child from three to six months of age will smile at human faces or reasonable facsimiles thereof. The face of the human being (or of a mask, even of a scarecrow) must however have two eyes, be fully visible, and show movement. It need not be a

8. R. A. Spitz and K. M. Wolf, The Smiling Response: A Contribution to the Ontogenesis of Social Relations, *Genetic Psychology Monograph, 34* (1946), 57–125.

24

smiling face (a fact that rules out imitation), nor need it belong to a familiar person. Strangers evoke a smile as readily as does the mother. After the age of six months, normally, the same perceptual pattern arouses the opposite response if the face is unfamiliar. Strangers provoke fear, not smiles. And, according to Spitz and Wolf, if the emotional relations between the child and its mother are seriously disturbed, the social smile fails to develop or shows abnormalities even within the three to six months' period. Now this type of work is exceedingly important, for it not only tells us about the raw dispositions that underlie human development but points to the fact that dispositions and their maturation depend upon the total concurrent state of becoming. In this case the child's social relations must be benign for the instinct to appear.

A second cluster of dispositions includes all that we normally call "inheritance"—those gene-linked characteristics we associate with family, stock, and race. Since combinations of gene-linked traits are apparently almost infinite in number, we note that this type of determination provides the basis for endless uniqueness in personality, even before the differential operations of culture and environment get under way. To be sure, genes account also for species uniformity, for our having two eyes, a backbone, and a standard equipment of glands. But when we speak of inheritance we are likely to think of similarities (e.g., of the child's resemblance to his parents) and to forget that the operation of genes also starts us well on the road to uniqueness, with our varying endowments of temperament, neural plasticity, and thresholds of response. Perhaps we forget this fact partly because

25

human genetics is so little understood (with its discoveries to date concentrated on types rather than individual patterns of inheritance), and partly because as devotees of the tabula rasa we do not choose to give full credit to the innate determinants of human nature.

There is yet a third and very different sense in which we may speak of original dispositions. It is not, so far as we know, a matter of specific gene determination or of instinct, except perhaps in the broadest possible sense. I refer to certain latent or potential capacities that play a crucial role in becoming. Every young animal, for example, seems to have the *capacity to learn*. That is to say, there is something inherently plastic in his neuropsychic nature that will make changes in response possible. If he is normally endowed the human infant will in time develop a conscience, a sense of self, and a hierarchical organization of traits. He will become some sort of structural system, self-regulating and self-maintaining. What is more, he will exert himself to become something more than a stencil copy of the species to which he belongs. Such capacities are not instincts in the sense of McDougall or Freud; rather they represent potentialities for attaining adulthood. What we call instincts are primarily means for ensuring survival: the capacities I speak of are of the sort to ensure growth and orderly structure. They bring about characteristic stadia in human development.

Consider for a moment the capacity to learn. No theory of motivation explains why we learn at all; at best it accounts for the urge but not for the modifiability of conduct. Nor does any so-called "learning theory" tell why we learn, but only how we learn. Everyone knows *that* we learn, but few psychologists, least of all the Lockeans, seem to wonder about the nature of the underlying disposition to adapt and to modify behavior. Now whatever else learning may be it is clearly *a disposition to form structures.* Such structures include simple habits and sequences of habits; but they also include more complex and less rigid structures such as moral conscience, one's conception of oneself, pre-emptive traits and interests, schemata of meaning, and even one's embracing philosophy of life. Up to now few concepts pertaining to learning give proper recognition to its structural nature. (Possible exceptions may be noted in the Gestalt doctrine of "closure" and in Thorndike's later assumption of "belongingness.") [9]

Learning, as it operates on instinct and inheritance, thus leads to the formation of more or less stable structures, among which we have listed the moral conscience, a self-concept, and a hierarchical organization of personality. But it would not do so unless these stadia too were carried in our natures as inherent possibilities. They likewise comprise a type of "given" in human nature, much neglected in personality theory today.

We maintain therefore that personality is governed not only by the impact of stimuli upon a slender endowment of drives common to the species. Its process of becoming is governed, as well, by a disposition to realize its possibilities, i.e., to become characteristically human at all stages of development. And one of the capacities most urgent is

9. The neglect of structural laws in science, particularly in the sciences of man, is discussed, with suggestive and constructive proposals, by F. H. Allport, *Theories of Perception and the Concept of Structure,* New York, Wiley, 1955; especially ch. 21.

individuation, the formation of an individual style of life that is self-aware, self-critical, and self-enhancing.

In this intricate process of growth we encounter the puzzling question: What is the relative importance of earlier and of later stages of development? We know that there are layers in each person that are archaic and composed of relatively isolated earlier systems. Yet there are also layers in which man is fully adult, his psychological maturity corresponding to his age. The drama of human life can be written largely in terms of the friction engendered between earlier stages and later stages of development. Becoming is the process of incorporating earlier stages into later; or when this is impossible, of handling the conflict between early and late stages as well as one can.

§ 7. Unsocial Beginnings

WHILE THE infant is a socially dependent being, he is not even to the slightest degree a socialized being. Even at the age of two the child is, when measured by standards applied to adults, an unsocialized horror. Picture, if you can, an adult who is extremely destructive of property, insistent and demanding that every desire be instantly gratified, helpless and almost totally dependent on others, unable to share his possessions, impatient, prone to tantrums, violent and uninhibited in the display of all his feelings. Such behavior, normal to a two-year-old, would be monstrous in a man. Unless these qualities are markedly altered in the process of becoming we have on our

28

hands an infantile and potentially evil personality. Hobbes well said that the wicked man is but a child grown strong.

The young child's striving is directed toward the immediate object, an object to eat, to play with, enjoy, avoid, or to love. The striving is impulsive, transitory, unreflective, and not referred to self. Its significance does not transcend the present moment. By contrast, mature striving is linked to long-range goals. Thus, the process of becoming is largely a matter of organizing transitory impulses into a pattern of striving and interest in which the element of self-awareness plays a large part.

We cannot know the young child's personality by studying his systems of interest, for his attention is as yet too labile, his reactions impulsive, and interests unformed. From adolescence onward, however, the surest clue to personality is the hierarchy of interests, including the loves and loyalties of adult life. When we know a person's *ordo amoris* we truly know that person.

It is obvious, then, that the primary problem in the psychology of becoming is to account for the transformation by which the unsocialized infant becomes an adult with structured loves, hates, loyalties, and interests, capable of taking his place in a complexly ordered society.

History is filled with proposed solutions to this problem. Often the issue is stated (somewhat too moralistically) in terms of egoism versus altruism. Some writers— among them Adam Smith, Giddings, Kropotkin, and Ashley Montagu—see in human nature the operation of innately socializing propensities, such as gregariousness, sympathy, imitation, or an instinct of mutual aid of a sort that guarantees in advance a measure of altruism in

29

the course of growth. But these alleged processes do little more than name the phenomenon in question and fail to offer a detailed account of the transformation. Other writers, by contrast, hold that man is never truly socialized. He remains a savage at heart, and his social varnish is superficial and thin. Hobbes, Nietzsche, Stirner, and Le Dantec are of this persuasion.[10]

As an over-all proposition, I submit, Comte's "law of affective evolution" comes nearer to the truth. This law holds that with time there comes a diminution in the preponderance and intensity of personal inclinations, and a growth and extension of other-regarding sentiments. To state it differently, the young infant, being totally unsocialized, cannot display any of the eventual structures of personality that require learning. His dependency-needs are bound up entirely with his immediate demands. True, he has a "disposition" for eventual socialization, yet the first stages of becoming are necessarily devoid of altruism. When, however, mediating structures of conscience, imagination, and extension of the ego develop, then genuine transformations of motivation may occur. In proportion as an individual is democratically socialized he finds it intolerable to seek happiness at the expense of others. Such transformation does not, of course, eliminate primary egoism altogether—not even in a saint. Self-love, it is obvious, remains always positive and active in our natures. Our theory holds only that it need not remain dominant.

10. A fuller account of these and other relevant theories is to be found in G. W. Allport, "Historical Background of Modern Social Psychology," ch. 1 in *A Handbook of Social Psychology*, ed. by G. Lindzey, Cambridge, Addison-Wesley, 1954.

∫ 8. The Importance of Early Affiliation

OUR PRINCIPAL problem then is to relate the earlier stages of becoming to the later. Freud taught that the foundations of character are established by the age of three; he held that while later events may be able to modify they can never basically alter the traits then formed.[11] Even Adler, who agrees with Freud on little else, dates the adoption of a lasting style of life around the age of four or five.[12]

While there is serious exaggeration in these views we dare not blind ourselves to the impressive supporting evidence that exists. We think in this connection of the work of Spitz, Levy, Anna Freud, and others. Bowlby has reviewed their investigations and added important data of his own.[13] With some regularity it turns out that a child's character and mental health depend to a considerable degree upon his relationship with his mother in early years. Adverse relationships seem often to create insuperable obstacles to effective therapeutic treatment at later periods of life. Delinquency, mental disorder, and ethnic prejudice are among the antisocial conditions that have been traced in part to affectional deprivation and disturb-

11. Cf. E. Jones, *The Life and Work of Sigmund Freud* (New York, Basic Books, 1953), p. 13.

12. Cf. A. Adler, *Problems of Neurosis* (New York, Cosmopolitan Book, 1930), p. 48.

13. J. Bowlby, "Maternal Care and Mental Health," *Bulletin of the World Health Organization, 3*, No. 3 (1951).

ance in early childhood.[14] All in all a generous minimum of security seems required in early years for a start toward a productive life-style. Without it the individual develops a pathological craving for security, and is less able than others to tolerate setbacks in maturity. Through his insistent demanding, jealousy, depredations, and egoism he betrays the craving that still haunts him. By contrast, the child who receives adequate gratification of his infant needs is more likely to be prepared to give up his habits of demanding, and to learn tolerance for his later frustrations. Having completed successfully one stage of development he is free to abandon the habits appropriate to this stage and to enter the mature reaches of becoming. Having known acceptance in an affectionate environment he learns more readily to accept himself, to tolerate the ways of the world, and to handle the conflicts of later life in a mature manner.[15]

If this interpretation is correct it means that early affiliative needs (dependence, succorance, and attachment) are the ground of becoming, even in their presocialized stages. They demand a basic rapport with the world before growth proper can start. Aggression and hatred, by contrast, are reactive protests, aroused only when affiliative tendencies are thwarted.[16] A patient in treatment, we know, makes progress toward health in proportion as his resentments, hostility, and hatred lessen,

14. This evidence is examined by G. W. Allport, *The Nature of Prejudice* (Cambridge, Addison-Wesley, 1954), chs. 18, 25.

15. This thesis is developed more fully in A. H. Maslow, *Motivation and Personality*, New York, Harper, 1954.

16. See P. A. Sorokin, ed., *Explorations in Altruistic Love and Behavior*, Boston, Beacon Press, 1950; *especially* ch. 5.

and in proportion as he feels accepted and wanted by therapist, family, and associates. Love received and love given comprise the best form of therapy. But love is not easily commanded or offered by one whose whole life has been marked by reactive protest against early deprivation.

It is a hopeful sign that psychologists are turning their attention to the affiliative groundwork of life. Its sheer ubiquity has perhaps led to its relative neglect up to now. We have paid more attention to the pathology of becoming than to its normal course, focusing upon disease rather than health, upon bad citizenship rather than good, and upon prejudice rather than tolerance and charity.

We are now, I think, in a position to evaluate the claim that the foundations of character are established by the age of three, four, or five years of age. The argument seems strong indeed that disordered affiliative relationships may leave an ineradicable scar. Pathological anxiety and also guilt in adult years may be nothing more than manifestations of unresolved infant distress. For this type of sufferer we may say that the process of becoming has been, in important respects, arrested in early life. But for the child who enjoys a normal affiliative groundwork, and who successfully enters the more advanced stages of socialization, the situation is different. In his case the foundations of character were established by the age of three or five, only in the sense that he is now *free to become;* he is not retarded; he is well launched on the course of continuous and unimpeded growth. I need not point out that this interpretation of the role of early years departs in important respects from the doctrine of psychoanalysis that views the character of healthy people, as well as the unhealthy, as fundamentally established by the age of three.

§ 9. Tribalism and Individuation

GRANTED that early security and affectional relationships are the ground of becoming, and granted too that in some cases ineradicable effects are established in the early years of life, we are still in possession of only one part of the truth.

While the child needs and wants love and security, he does not want them to interfere with his impulses, his freedom, or his preferred ways of acting. From the very start of his life he is resistant to the smothering effects of his social environment. Affiliation alone would make for slavish obedience to family or tribal living which provide the child with his early standards of conduct and with his definitions of the world around him. If these influences were the only ones acting upon him they would lead to conduct always conventional and stereotyped. It is a limitation of current theories of socialization that they do in fact deal only with the mirror-like character of the so-called superego, that they tend to define socialization exclusively in terms of conformity, and not also in terms of creative becoming.

The truth of the matter, however, is that the moral sense and life-styles of most people reach far beyond the confines of domestic and community mores in which they were first fashioned. If we look into ourselves we observe that our tribal morality seems to us somehow peripheral to our personal integrity. True, we obey conventions of modesty, decorum, and self-control, and have many habits that fashion us in part as mirror-images of our home, class, and cultural ways of living. But we know that we have selected, reshaped, and transcended these ways to a marked degree.

Thus there seem to be two contrary forces at work. The one makes for a closed tribal being. It takes its start in the dependence of the child upon those who care for him. His gratifications and his security come from the outside; so too do all the first lessons he learns: the times of day when he may have meals, the activities for which he is punished and those that bring reward. He is coerced and cajoled into conformity but not, we note, with complete success. He shows a capacity even from birth to resist the impact of maternal and tribal demands. While to a certain degree his group shapes his course, at the same time it seems to antagonize him, as if he realized its threat to his integrity.

If the demand for autonomy were not a major force we could not explain the prominence of negativistic behavior in childhood. The crying, rejecting, and anger of a young infant as well as the negativistic behavior of the two-year-old are primitive indications of a being bent on asserting itself. All his life long this being will be attempting to reconcile these two modes of becoming, the tribal and the personal: the one that makes him into a mirror, the other that lights the lamp of individuality within.[17]

17. This antinomy is the basis of Henri Bergson's treatise, *The Two Sources of Morality and Religion,* trans. by R. A. Audra and C. Brereton, New York, Henry Holt, 1935.

§ 10. Is the Concept of Self Necessary?

WE COME now to a question that is pivotal for the psychology of growth: Is the concept of *self* necessary? While there is a vast literature in philosophy devoted to this issue from the points of view of ontology, epistemology, and axiology, let us for the time being by-pass such discussions. For it is entirely conceivable that a concept useful to philosophy or theology may turn out to be merely an impediment in the path of psychological progress.

Since the time of Wundt, the central objection of psychology to *self*, and also to *soul*, has been that the concept seems question-begging. It is temptingly easy to assign functions that are not fully understood to a mysterious central agency, and then to declare that "it" performs in such a way as to unify the personality and maintain its integrity. Wundt, aware of this peril, declared boldly for "a psychology without a soul." It was not that he necessarily denied philosophical or theological postulates, but that he felt psychology as science would be handicapped by the *petitio principii* implied in the concept. For half a century few psychologists other than Thomists have resisted Wundt's reasoning or his example.[18] Indeed we may

18. Until about 1890 certain American writers, including Dewey, Royce, James, continued to regard self as a necessary concept. They felt that the analytical concepts of the New Psychology lost the manifest unity of mental functioning. But for the ensuing fifty years very few American psychologists made use of it, Mary Whiton Calkins being a distinguished exception; and none employed "soul." *See* G. W. Allport, "The Ego in Contemporary Psychology," *Psychological Review,* 50 (1943), 451–78; reprinted in *The Nature of Personality: Selected Papers,* Cambridge, Addison-Wesley, 1950.

say that for two generations psychologists have tried every conceivable way of accounting for the integration, organization, and striving of the human person without having recourse to the postulate of a self.

In very recent years the tide has turned. Perhaps without being fully aware of the historical situation, many psychologists have commenced to embrace what two decades ago would have been considered a heresy. They have reintroduced self and ego unashamedly and, as if to make up for lost time, have employed ancillary concepts such as *self-image, self-actualization, self-affirmation, phenomenal ego, ego-involvement, ego-striving,* and many other hyphenated elaborations which to experimental positivism still have a slight flavor of scientific obscenity.

We should note in passing that Freud played a leading, if unintentional role, in preserving the concept of ego from total obliteration throughout two generations of strenuous positivism. His own use of the term, to be sure, shifted. At first he spoke of assertive and aggressive ego-instincts (in a Nietzschean sense); later for Freud the ego became a rational, though passive, agency, whose duty it was to reconcile as best it could through planning or defense the conflicting pressures of the instincts, of conscience, and of the outer environment. With the core concept thus preserved, even with stringently limited meanings, it was easier for dynamically inclined psychologists, including the neo-Freudians, to enlarge the properties of the ego, making it a far more active and important agent than it was in the hands of Freud.

There still remains, however, the danger that Wundt wished to avoid, namely that the ego may be regarded as a *deus ex machina,* invoked to reassemble the dismembered parts of the throbbing psychic machine after positivism

37

has failed to do so. The situation today seems to be that many psychologists who first fit personality to an external set of co-ordinates are dissatisfied with the result. They therefore re-invent the ego because they find no coherence among the measures yielded by positivistic analysis. But unfortunately positivism and ego-theory do not go well together. Bergson has criticized the use of "ego" in this face-saving way by likening the process to the dilemma of an artist. An artist, he says, may wish to represent Paris—just as a psychologist may wish to represent personality. But all he can do with the limitations of his medium is to draw this and then that angle of the whole. To each sketch he applies the label "Paris," hoping somehow that the sections he has ablated will magically reconstitute the whole.[19] Similarly in psychology we have a state of affairs where empiricists, finding that they have gone as far as possible with analytic tools and being dissatisfied with the product, resort as did their predecessors to some concept of self in order to represent, however inadequately, the coherence, unity, and purposiveness they know they have lost in their fragmentary representations.

I greatly fear that the lazy tendency to employ self or ego as a factotum to repair the ravages of positivism may do more harm than good. It is, of course, significant that so many contemporary psychologists feel forced to take this step, even though for the most part their work represents no theoretical gain over nineteenth-century usage. Positivism will continue to resent the intrusion, and will, with some justification, accuse today's resurgent self-psychologists of obscurantism.

19. H. Bergson, *Introduction to Metaphysics* (New York, G. Putnam's Sons, 1912), p. 30.

The problem then becomes how to approach the phenomena that have led to a revival of the self-concept in a manner that will advance rather than retard scientific progress.

A possible clue to the solution, so far as psychology is concerned, lies in a statement made by Alfred Adler. "What is frequently labeled 'the ego,'" he writes, "is nothing more than the style of the individual." [20] Life-style to Adler had a deep and important meaning. He is saying that if psychology could give us a full and complete account of life-style it would automatically include all phenomena now referred somewhat vaguely to a self or an ego. In other words, a wholly adequate psychology of growth would discover all of the activities and all of the interrelations in life, which are now either neglected or consigned to an ego that looks suspiciously like a homunculus.

The first thing an adequate psychology of growth should do is to draw a distinction between what are matters of *importance* to the individual and what are, as Whitehead would say, merely matters of *fact* to him; that is, between what he feels to be vital and central in becoming and what belongs to the periphery of his being.

Many facets of our life-style are not ordinarily felt to have strong personal relevance. Each of us, for example, has innumerable tribal habits that mark our life-style but are nothing more than opportunistic modes of adjusting. The same holds true for many of our physiological habits. We keep to the right in traffic, obey the rules of etiquette,

20. A. Adler, "The Fundamental Views of Individual Psychology," *International Journal of Individual Psychology, 1* (1935), 5–8.

and make countless unconscious or semiconscious adjustments, all of which characterize our life-style but are not *propriate,* i.e., not really central to our sense of existence. Consider, for example, the English language habits that envelop our thinking and communication. Nothing could be of more pervasive influence in our lives than the store of concepts available to us in our ancestral tongue and the frames of discourse under which our social contacts proceed. And yet the use of English is ordinarily felt to be quite peripheral to the core of our existence. It would not be so if some foreign invader should forbid us to use our native language. At such a time our vocabulary and accent and our freedom to employ them would become very precious and involved with our sense of self. So it is with the myriad of social and physiological habits we have developed that are never, unless interfered with, regarded as essential to our existence as a separate being.

Personality includes these habits and skills, frames of reference, matters of fact and cultural values, that seldom or never seem warm and important. But personality includes what is warm and important also—all the regions of our life that we regard as peculiarly ours, and which for the time being I suggest we call the *proprium.* The proprium includes all aspects of personality that make for inward unity.

Psychologists who allow for the proprium use both the term "self" and "ego"—often interchangeably; and both terms are defined with varying degrees of narrowness or of comprehensiveness. Whatever name we use for it, this sense of what is "peculiarly ours" merits close scrutiny.

40

THE PROPRIUM

The principal functions and properties of the proprium need to be distinguished. *the science or technique of classification*

To this end William James over sixty years ago proposed a simple taxonomic scheme.[21] There are, he maintained, two possible orders of self: an empirical self (the *Me*) and a knowing self (the *I*). Three subsidiary types comprise the empirical Me: the material self, the social self, and the spiritual self. Within this simple framework he fits his famous and subtle description of the various states of mind that are "peculiarly ours." His scheme, however, viewed in the perspective of modern psychoanalytic and experimental research, seems scarcely adequate. In particular it lacks the full psychodynamic flavor of modern thinking. With some trepidation, therefore, I offer what I hope is an improved outline for analyzing the propriate aspects of personality. Later we shall return to the question, Is the concept of *self* necessary?

§ 11. The Proprium

1. *Bodily sense.* The first aspect we encounter is the bodily *me*. It seems to be composed of streams of sensations that arise within the organism—from viscera, muscles, tendons, joints, vestibular canals, and other regions of the body. The technical name for the bodily sense is *coenesthesis*. Usually this sensory stream is experienced dimly; often we are totally unaware of it. At times, how-

21. *Principles of Psychology.* (New York, Henry Holt, 1890), *1*, ch. 10.

ever, it is well configurated in consciousness in the exhilaration that accompanies physical exercise, or in moments of sensory delight or pain. The infant, apparently, does not know that such experiences are "his." But they surely form a necessary foundation for his emerging sense of self. The baby who at first cries from unlocalized discomfort will, in the course of growth, show progressive ability to identify the distress as his own.

The bodily sense remains a lifelong anchor for our self-awareness, though it never alone accounts for the entire sense of self, probably not even in the young child who has his memories, social cues, and strivings to help in the definition. Psychologists have paid a great deal of attention, however, to this particular component of self-awareness, rather more than to other equally important ingredients. One special line of investigation has been surprisingly popular: the attempt to locate self in relation to specific bodily sensations. When asked, some people will say that they *feel* the self in their right hands, or in the viscera. Most, however, seem to agree with Claparède that a center midway between the eyes, slightly behind them within the head, is the focus. It is from this cyclopean eye that we estimate what lies before and behind ourselves, to the right or left, and above and below. Here, phenomenologically speaking, is the locus of the ego.[22] Interesting as this type of work may be, it represents

22. E. Claparede, "Note sur la localisation du moi," *Archives de psychologie, 19* (1924), 172–82.

Another school of thought has placed considerable stress upon the total body-image. Its variations are said to mark changes in the course of development. Schilder, for example, points out that in experience of hate the body-image itself contracts; in experience of

little more than the discovery that various sensory elements in the coenesthetic stream or various inferences drawn from sensory experience may for certain people at certain times be especially prominent.

How very intimate (propriate) the bodily sense is can be seen by performing a little experiment in your imagination. Think first of swallowing the saliva in your mouth, or do so. Then imagine expectorating it into a tumbler and drinking it! What seemed natural and "mine" suddenly becomes disgusting and alien. Or picture yourself sucking blood from a prick in your finger; then imagine sucking blood from a bandage around your finger! What I perceive as belonging intimately to my body is warm and welcome; what I perceive as separate from my body becomes, in the twinkling of an eye, cold and foreign.

Certainly organic sensations, their localization and recognition, composing as they do the bodily *me*, are a core of becoming. But it would be a serious mistake to think, as some writers do, that they alone account for our sense of what is "peculiarly ours."

2. *Self-identity.* Today I remember some of my thoughts of yesterday; and tomorrow I shall remember some of my thoughts of both yesterday and today; and I am subjectively certain that they are the thoughts of the same person. In this situation, no doubt, the organic continuity of the neuromuscular system is the leading factor. Yet the process involves more than reminiscence made

love it expands, and even seems phenomenally to include other beings. See P. Schilder, *The Image and Appearance of the Human Body*, Psyche Monograph (London, K. Paul, Trench, Trubner Co., 1935), p. 353.

possible by our retentive nerves. The young infant has retentive capacity during the first months of life but in all probability no sense of self-identity. This sense seems to grow gradually, partly as a result of being clothed and named, and otherwise marked off from the surrounding environment. Social interaction is an important factor. It is the actions of the other to which he differentially adjusts that force upon a child the realization that he is not the other, but a being in his own right. The difficulty of developing self-identity in childhood is shown by the ease with which a child depersonalizes himself in play and in speech.[23] Until the age of four or five we have good reason to believe that as perceived by the child personal identity is unstable. Beginning at about this age, however, it becomes the surest attest a human being has of his own existence.

3. *Ego-enhancement.* We come now to the most notorious property of the proprium, to its unabashed self-seeking.[24] Scores of writers have featured this clamorous trait in human personality. It is tied to the need for survival, for it is easy to see that we are endowed by nature with the impulses of self-assertion and with the emotions of self-satisfaction and pride. Our language is laden with evidence. The commonest compound of self is *selfish,* and

23. Cf. G. W. Allport, *Personality. A Psychological Interpretation* (New York, Henry Holt, 1937), pp. 159–65.

24. The term "proprium" was a favorite of Emanuel Swedenborg. He used it, however, in the narrow sense of selfishness and pride, a meaning that corresponds here fairly closely to "ego-enhancement." See his *Proprium,* with an introduction by John Bigelow, New York, New Church Board of Publication, 1907. I am grateful to Professor Howard D. Spoerl for his clarification of this matter.

of ego *egoism*. Pride, humiliation, self-esteem, narcissism are such prominent factors that when we speak of ego or self we often have in mind only this aspect of personality. And yet, self-love may be prominent in our natures without necessarily being sovereign. The proprium, as we shall see, has other facets and functions.

4. *Ego-extension.* The three facets we have discussed—coenesthesis, self-identity, ego-enhancement—are relatively early developments in personality, characterizing the whole of the child's proprium. Their solicitations have a heavily biological quality and seem to be contained within the organism itself. But soon the process of learning brings with it a high regard for possessions, for loved objects, and later, for ideal causes and loyalties. We are speaking here of whatever objects a person calls "mine." They must at the same time be objects of *importance,* for sometimes our sense of "having" has no affective tone and hence no place in the proprium. A child, however, who identifies with his parent is definitely extending his sense of self, as he does likewise through his love for pets, dolls, or other possessions, animate or inanimate.

As we grow older we identify with groups, neighborhood, and nation as well as with possessions, clothes, home. They become matters of importance to us in a sense that other people's families, nations, or possessions are not. Later in life the process of extension may go to great lengths, through the development of loyalties and of interests focused on abstractions and on moral and religious values. Indeed, a mark of maturity seems to be the range and extent of one's feeling of self-involvement in abstract ideals.

5. *Rational agent.* The ego, according to Freud, has the

task of keeping the organism as a whole in touch with reality, of intermediating between unconscious impulses and the outer world. Often the rational ego can do little else than invent and employ defenses to forestall or diminish anxiety. These protective devices shape the development of personality to an extent unrealized sixty years ago. It is thanks to Freud that we understand the strategies of denial, repression, displacement, reaction formation, rationalization, and the like better than did our ancestors.

We have become so convinced of the validity of these defense mechanisms, and so impressed with their frequency of operation, that we are inclined to forget that the rational functioning of the proprium is capable also of yielding true solutions, appropriate adjustments, accurate planning, and a relatively faultless solving of the equations of life.

Many philosophers, dating as far back as Boethius in the sixth century, have seen the rational nature of personality as its most distinctive property. (*Persona est substantia individua rationalis naturae.*) It may seem odd to credit Freud, the supreme irrationalist of our age, with helping the Thomists preserve for psychology the emphasis upon the ego as the rational agent in personality, but such is the case. For whether the ego reasons or merely rationalizes, it has the property of synthesizing inner needs and outer reality. Freud and the Thomists have not let us forget this fact, and have thus made it easier for modern cognitive theories to deal with this central function of the proprium.

6. *Self-image.* A propriate function of special interest today is the self-image, or as some writers call it, the phe-

46

nomenal self. Present-day therapy is chiefly devoted to leading the patient to examine, correct, or expand this self-image. The image has two aspects: the way the patient regards his present abilities, status, and roles; and what he would like to become, his *aspirations* for himself. The latter aspect, which Karen Horney calls the "idealized self-image," [25] is of especial importance in therapy. On the one hand it may be compulsive, compensatory, and un-realistic, blinding its possessor to his true situation in life. On the other hand, it may be an insightful cognitive map, closely geared to reality and defining a wholesome ambi-tion. The ideal self-image is the imaginative aspect of the proprium, and whether accurate or distorted, attainable or unattainable, it plots a course by which much pro-priate movement is guided and therapeutic progress achieved.

There are, of course, many forms of becoming that re-quire no self-image, including automatic cultural learn-ing and our whole repertoire of opportunistic adjust-ments to our environment. Yet there is also much growth that takes place only with the aid of, and because of, a self-image. This image helps us bring our view of the present into line with our view of the future. Fortunately the dy-namic importance of the self-image is more widely recog-nized in psychology today than formerly.

7. *Propriate striving.* We come now to the nature of motivation. Unfortunately we often fail to distinguish between propriate and peripheral motives. The reason is that at the rudimentary levels of becoming, which up to now have been the chief levels investigated, it *is* the im-

25. Karen Horney, *Neurosis and Human Growth: The Struggle toward Self-realization,* New York, Norton, 1950.

pulses and drives, the immediate satisfaction and tension reduction, that are the determinants of conduct. Hence a psychology of opportunistic adjustment seems basic and adequate, especially to psychologists accustomed to working with animals. At low levels of behavior the familiar formula of drives and their conditioning appears to suffice. But as soon as the personality enters the stage of ego-extension, and develops a self-image with visions of self-perfection, we are, I think, forced to postulate motives of a different order, motives that reflect propriate striving. Within experimental psychology itself there is now plenty of evidence that conduct that is "ego involved" (propriate) differs markedly from behavior that is not.[26]

Many psychologists disregard this evidence. They wish to maintain a single theory of motivation consistent with their presuppositions. Their preferred formula is in terms of drive and conditioned drive. Drive is viewed as a peripherally instigated activity. The resultant response is simply reactive, persisting only until the instigator is removed and the tension, created by the drive, lessened. Seeking always a parsimony of assumptions, this view therefore holds that motivation entails one and only one inherent property of the organism: a disposition to act, by instinct or by learning, in such a way that the organism will as efficiently as possible reduce the discomfort of tension. Motivation is regarded as a state of tenseness that leads us to seek equilibrium, rest, adjustment, satisfaction, or homeostasis. From this point of view personality is nothing more than our habitual modes of reduc-

26. Cf. G. W. Allport, "The Ego in Contemporary Psychology," *Psychological Review*, 50 (1943), 451–78.

ing tension. This formulation, of course, is wholly consistent with empiricism's initial presupposition that man is by nature a passive being, capable only of receiving impressions from, and responding to, external goads.

The contrary view holds that this formula, while applicable to segmental and opportunistic adjustments, falls short of representing the nature of propriate striving. It points out that the characteristic feature of such striving is its resistance to equilibrium: tension is maintained rather than reduced.

In his autobiography Raold Amundsen tells how from the age of fifteen he had one dominant passion—to become a polar explorer. The obstacles seemed insurmountable, and all through his life the temptations to reduce the tensions engendered were great. But the propriate striving persisted. While he welcomed each success, it acted to raise his level of aspiration, to maintain an over-all commitment. Having sailed the Northwest Passage, he embarked upon the painful project that led to the discovery of the South Pole. Having discovered the South Pole, he planned for years, against extreme discouragement, to fly over the North Pole, a task he finally accomplished. But his commitment never wavered until at the end he lost his life in attempting to rescue a less gifted explorer, Nobile, from death in the Arctic. Not only did he maintain one style of life, without ceasing, but this central commitment enabled him to withstand the temptation to reduce the segmental tensions continually engendered by fatigue, hunger, ridicule, and danger.[27]

Here we see the issue squarely. A psychology that re-

27. Raold Amundsen, *My Life as an Explorer*, Garden City, N.Y., Doubleday, Doran, 1928.

gards motivation exclusively in terms of drives and conditioned drives is likely to stammer and grow vague when confronted by those aspects of personality—of every personality—that resemble Amundsen's propriate striving. While most of us are less distinguished than he in our achievements, we too have insatiable interests. Only in a very superficial way can these interests be dealt with in terms of tension reduction. Many writers past and present have recognized this fact and have postulated some principles of an exactly opposite order. One thinks in this connection of Spinoza's concept of conatus, or the tendency of an individual to persist, against obstacles, in his own style of being. One thinks of Goldstein's doctrine of *self-actualization,* used also by Maslow and others, or McDougall's *self-regarding* sentiment. And one thinks too of those modern Freudians who feel the need for endowing the ego not only with a rational and rationalizing ability but with a tendency to maintain its own system of productive interests, in spite of the passing solicitations of impulse and environmental instigation. Indeed the fortified ego, as described by neo-Freudians, is able to act contrary to the usual course of opportunistic, tension-reducing, adaptation.

Propriate striving distinguishes itself from other forms of motivation in that, however beset by conflicts, it makes for unification of personality. There is evidence that the lives of mental patients are marked by the proliferation of unrelated subsystems, and by the loss of more homogeneous systems of motivation.[28] When the individual is dominated by segmental drives, by compulsions, or by the

28. Cf. L. McQuitty, "A Measure of Personality Integration in Relation to the Concept of the Self," *Journal of Personality, 18* (1950), 461–82.

winds of circumstance, he has lost the integrity that comes only from maintaining major directions of striving. The possession of long-range goals, regarded as central to one's personal existence, distinguishes the human being from the animal, the adult from the child, and in many cases the healthy personality from the sick.

Striving, it is apparent, always has a future reference. As a matter of fact, a great many states of mind are adequately described only in terms of their futurity. Along with *striving*, we may mention *interest, tendency, disposition, expectation, planning, problem solving,* and *intention*. While not all future-directedness is phenomenally propriate, it all requires a type of psychology that transcends the prevalent tendency to explain mental states exclusively in terms of past occurrences. People, it seems, are busy leading their lives into the future, whereas psychology, for the most part, is busy tracing them into the past.

8. *The knower.* Now that we have isolated these various propriate functions—all of which we regard as peculiarly ours—the question arises whether we are yet at an end. Do we not have in addition a cognizing self—a knower, that transcends all other functions of the proprium and holds them in view? In a famous passage, William James wrestles with this question, and concludes that we have not. There is, he thinks, no such thing as a substantive self distinguishable from the sum total, or stream, of experiences. Each moment of consciousness, he says, appropriates each previous moment, and the knower is thus somehow embedded in what is known. "The thoughts themselves are the thinker." [29]

Opponents of James argue that no mere series of expe-

29. *Principles of Psychology, 1,* ch. 10.

riences can possibly turn themselves into an awareness of that series as a unit. Nor can "passing thoughts" possibly regard themselves as important or interesting. To whom is the series important or interesting if not to *me?* I am the ultimate monitor. The self as *knower* emerges as a final and inescapable postulate.

It is interesting to ask why James balked at admitting a knowing self after he had so lavishly admitted to psychology with his full approval material, social, and spiritual selves. The reason may well have been (and the reason would be valid today) that one who laboriously strives to depict the nature of propriate functions on an empirical level, hoping thereby to enrich the science of psychology with a discriminating analysis of self, is not anxious to risk a return to the homunculus theory by introducing a synthesizer, or a self of selves.

To be sure, the danger that abuse might follow the admission of a substantive knower into the science of psychology is no reason to avoid this step if it is logically required. Some philosophers, including Kant, insist that the pure or transcendental ego is separable from the empirical ego (i.e., from any of the propriate states thus far mentioned).[30] Those who hold that the knowing itself is not (as James argued) merely an aspect of the self as

30. Kant's position on this matter is summarized in the following pronouncement: "One may therefore say of the thinking I (the soul), which represents itself as substance, simple, numerically identical in all time, and as the correlative of all existence, from which in fact all other existence must be concluded, that it *does not know itself through the categories,* but knows the *categories* only, and through them all objects, in the absolute unity of apperception, *that is through itself." Critique of Pure Reason,* trans. by M. Müller (London, Macmillan, 1881), p. 347.

known, but is 'pure' and 'transcendental,' argue, as Kant does, that the texture of knowledge is quite different in the two cases. Our cognition of our knowing self is always indirect, of the order of a presupposition. On the other hand, all features of the *empirical self* are known directly, through acquaintance, as any object is known which falls into time and space categories.[31]

While their metaphysical positions are directly opposed, both Kant and James agree with their illustrious predecessor, Descartes, that the knowing function is a vital attribute of the self however defined. For our present purpose this is the point to bear in mind.

We not only know *things,* but we know (i.e., are acquainted with) the empirical features of our own proprium. It is I who have bodily sensations, I who recognize my self-identity from day to day; I who note and reflect upon my self-assertion, self-extension, my own rationalizations, as well as upon my interests and strivings. When I thus think about my own propriate functions I am likely to perceive their essential togetherness, and feel them intimately bound in some way to the knowing function itself.

Since such knowing is, beyond any shadow of doubt, a state that is peculiarly ours, we admit it as the eighth clear function of the proprium. (In other words, as an eighth valid meaning of "self" or "ego.") But it is surely one of nature's perversities that so central a function should be so little understood by science, and should remain a perpetual bone of contention among philosophers. Many,

31. For a fuller discussion of this matter see F. R. Tennant, *Philosophical Theology* (Cambridge, University Press, 1928), *1,* ch. 5.

like Kant, set this function (the "pure ego") aside as something qualitatively apart from other propriate functions (the latter being assigned to the "empirical me"). Others, like James, say that the ego *qua* knower is somehow contained within the ego *qua* known. Still others, personalistically inclined, find it necessary to postulate a single self as knower, thinker, feeler, and doer—all in one blended unit of a sort that guarantees the continuance of all becoming.[32]

WE RETURN now to our unanswered question: Is the concept of self necessary in the psychology of personality? Our answer cannot be categorical since all depends upon the particular usage of "self" that is proposed. Certainly all legitimate phenomena that have been, and can be ascribed, to the self or ego must be admitted as data indispensable to a psychology of personal becoming. All eight functions of the "proprium" (our temporary neutral term for central interlocking operations of personality) must be admitted and included. In particular the unifying act of perceiving and knowing (of comprehending propriate states as belonging together and belonging to me) must be fully admitted.

At the same time, the danger we have several times warned against is very real: that a homunculus may creep into our discussions of personality, and be expected to solve all our problems without in reality solving any. Thus, if we ask "What determines our moral conduct?" the answer may be "The self does it." Or, if we pose the

32. P. A. Bertocci, "The Psychological Self, the Ego, and Personality," *Psychological Review*, 52 (1945), 91–9.

problem of choice, we say "The self chooses." Such question-begging would immeasurably weaken the scientific study of personality by providing an illegitimate regressus. There are, to be sure, ultimate problems of philosophy and of theology that psychology cannot even attempt to solve, and for the solution of such problems "self" in some restricted and technical meaning may be a necessity.

But so far as psychology is concerned our position, in brief, is this: all psychological functions commonly ascribed to a self or ego must be admitted as data in the scientific study of personality. These functions are not, however, coextensive with personality as a whole. They are rather the special aspects of personality that have to do with warmth, with unity, with a sense of personal importance. In this exposition I have called them "propriate" functions. If the reader prefers, he may call them self-functions, and in this sense self may be said to be a necessary psychological concept. What is unnecessary and inadmissible is a self (or soul) that is said to perform acts, to solve problems, to steer conduct, in a transpsychological manner, inaccessible to psychological analysis.

Once again we refer to Adler's contention that an adequate psychology of life-style would in effect dispense with the need for a separate psychology of the ego. I believe Adler's position, though unelaborated, is essentially the same as the one here advocated. An adequate psychology would in effect *be* a psychology of the ego. It would deal fully and fairly with propriate functions. Indeed, everyone would assume that psychology was talking about self-functions, unless it was expressly stated that peripheral, opportunistic, or actuarial events were under discussion. But as matters stand today, with so much of psychology preoccupied (as was Hume) with bits and pieces of experience, or else with generalized mathematical equations, it becomes necessary for the few psychologists who are concerned with propriate functions to specify in their discourse that they are dealing with them. If the horizons of psychology were more spacious than they are I venture to suggest that theories of personality would not need the concept of self or of ego except in certain compound forms, such as *self-knowledge, self-image, ego-enhancement, ego-extension.*

§ 12. The Fusion of Propriate Functions

IN DISTINGUISHING various functions of the proprium —bodily sense, self-identity, ego-enhancement, ego-extension, rational activity, self-image, propriate striving, and knowing—I hope I have not implied that any concrete instance of becoming may be explained by one and only one function. The fact is that at every stage of becoming a fusion of these functions is involved.

Take, for example, the acquiring of *self-insight* or *self-objectification,* one of the most important characteristics of maturity in personality. Here obviously is a condition where the knowing aspect of the proprium is engaged. It catches a glimpse of the rational processes, including those devoted to ego-defensiveness. At the same time the rational processes are evaluated in terms of the sense of importance (propriate striving). The self-image and the ideals resident in the extended ego play their part. It is not unlikely that the tangled process will arouse one's sense of humor, if one has it. Humor is a remarkable gift of perspective by which the knowing function of a mature person recognizes disproportions and absurdities within the proprium in the course of its encounters with the world.

In this particular case, the knowing function receives heavy emphasis, for the illustration happens to deal with the *cognition* of propriate states. But in other instances, the rational (or rationalizing) function may be more deeply involved, as in acts of insightful problem-solving, where the person is not primarily self-conscious but is simply finding a solution to some riddle of importance to him. In other instances self-assertion, acts of love, or carrying through a propriate purpose are in the ascendancy. But in all cases the functions are inextricably interlocked. The locus of the act is the person.

One common error in psychology is to center attention upon only one propriate function and attribute to it all, or nearly all, of the process of becoming. Thus Nietzscheans would fix upon the lust for power (self-assertion), Thomists upon the rational function, psychoanalysis upon the striving (particularly that portion that is not accessible to the knowing function). Some psychotherapists are occupied chiefly with the self-image (what the knowing function makes of the remainder of the proprium). We have already noted that some psychologists are concerned only with the coenesthetic components. Scholars interested in culture and personality deal primarily with the function of ego-extension, for their task is to account for the process of socialization. The truth of the matter is that all functions are important, and to center upon a portion of becoming that depends upon one function alone is to deliver a one-sided picture of growth in human personality.

But it is better to deal with propriate functions one-sidedly than not to deal with them at all. We have already seen that a large part of modern psychology, following the lead of Hume, denies that self or ego, in any sense whatsoever, forms a problem for the psychology of becoming. Habits and perceptions are treated as though they had separate existences, or else only the most inadequate "glue" is provided to account for the continuity and structure in personal development.

§ 13. Critique

LET US consider one suggestion made by psychologists who decline to recognize any special problem in accounting for propriate activity. The suggestion is that the concept of *emotion* suffices to our need. In place of "ego-involved acts" is it not sufficient to speak merely of "emotional acts?" [33] It is argued that psychology has always admitted more warmth and more self-consciousness under conditions of emotional arousal. Therefore in speaking of propriate versus peripheral behavior we may be dealing merely with emotional versus nonemotional behavior.

The proposal, I fear, is far from adequate. Propriate states are by no means always agitated states. A sense of

33. O. H. Mowrer, "The Law of Effect and Ego Psychology," *Psychological Review, 53* (1946), 321-34.

worthwhileness, of interest, of importance is not what we ordinarily call emotion. Each lasting sentiment in personality is a propriate state, but only on occasion does a sentiment erupt into emotion. An Amundsen planning for decades to fly over the North Pole is constantly ego-involved but rarely agitated. It is true that all propriate striving is felt to be important and laden with value—in this sense it is an affective state; but the sense of warmth and importance makes for efficiency and unity, not for the disruption and disintegration that often accompany emotional excitement.

There is considerable experimental evidence that bears on this matter. In the course of learning, for example, we know that high intensities of emotional excitement tend to narrow the field of learning, to reduce the effectiveness of cues, and to diminish the range of similarity and transfer.[34] Propriate involvement, on the other hand, increases the breadth of learning, of transfer effects, as well as the ability of the individual to perceive and organize all relevant information into the system as a whole.[35] Thus, the experimental effects of emotionality and of propriate involvement may be precisely opposite. We cannot, therefore, permit the two conditions to be confused in our theory of becoming.

The distinction is apparent in yet another way. We sometimes experience emotions without viewing them as having appreciable personal significance. A loud noise may evoke startle and bring in its train widespread vis-

34. D. A. Prescott, *Emotion and the Educative Process*, Washington, *American Council on Education,* 1938.

35. G. W. Allport, "The Ego in Contemporary Psychology," *Psychological Review, 50* (1943), 451–78.

ceral disturbance, without at the same time engaging to any appreciable extent our propriate functions. Pain suffered in a dentist chair is intense but may be less ego-involved than, let us say, a mild reproach from a friend. According to Bettelheim the most acute suffering in concentration camps, with its many poignant emotions, was often regarded as ego-alien, as something happening to one's body but not to one's person.[36] Even if we doubt that intense emotional experience can ever be totally devoid of a sense of self-involvement, we must at least concede that there is far from perfect correlation between them, and that therefore we should regard emotionality and the proprium as separable phenomena.

I have pressed this point because I wish to show that an adequate psychology of becoming cannot be written exclusively in terms of stimulus, emotional excitement, association, and response. It requires subjective and inner principles of organization of the sort frequently designated by the terms self or ego. Whether these labels are employed is less important than that the principles they imply be fully admitted in accounting for the development of personality.

THE POSITION I have attempted to defend is vulnerable to attack from precisely the opposite direction. Personalists will say that at every step our exposition has *assumed* the existence of a self or ego. Is not "proprium" a mere synonym for self? When one speaks of person, indi-

36. B. Bettelheim, "The Individual and Mass Behavior in Extreme Situations," *Journal of Abnormal and Social Psychology, 38* (1943), 417–52.

vidual, life-style, is not the self lurking therein? Can there be continuity in becoming without a continuing substance? When we speak of a sense of importance, who is the appraiser, if not the self?

These questions are clearly legitimate, and in a limited sense the implied accusation is justified. If we are accused of offering only a somewhat novel and differentiated doctrine of the self, we shall not deny the charge—provided the following novelties (as contrasted with most personalistic conceptions) are noted:

1. Person and personality are far broader conceptions than proprium. As we shall soon see, personality includes besides propriate functions a wide variety of adjustive activities, characteristic of the person and rendering the human organism the unique unit that it is. Many doctrines of self are so inclusive as to blur these distinctions.

2. Our position is that at birth we start with an organism (or individual) which develops unique modes of adjusting to and mastering the environment; these modes constitute personality. The earlier modes cannot involve propriate functions, though by the age of two or three they begin to do so.

3. The proprium is not a thing; it is not separable from the person as a whole. Above all it is not a homunculus. Proprium is a term intended to cover those functions that make for the peculiar unity and distinctiveness of personality, and at the same time seem to the knowing function to be subjectively intimate and important. The person is thus an individual organism capable of propriate activities, including, of course, the function of knowing.

4. The proprium develops in time. While we may grant that each human being has a disposition (capacity)

to develop a proprium, we stress the interlocking and emergent aspects of development rather than an unchanging nuclear self. Learning and socialization are major problems in the psychological view of becoming, whereas they recede into vagueness in most personalistic philosophies.

5. It is entirely conceivable, indeed probable, that an acceptable philosophy or theology of the person may logically require the concept of self to indicate the considerations of value and ontology important to a system of thought. It is partly to allow for this contingency that we have introduced the concept of proprium. It is a device to avoid trespassing upon, and confusion with, philosophical concepts that deal with somewhat different matters than does the psychological study of personality.

§ 14. Chance, Opportunistic, and Oriented Becoming

THE COURSE of growth, as we have said, is only in part guided by propriate functions. It is likewise in part random, and in part opportunistic. Among the random or chance factors we include those gene-linked dispositions that we group under the term "inheritance"; these are productive of temperament, motility, physique, and intelligence—all ground-conditions of personality—which, so far as we know, can be neither accurately predicted nor controlled. Chance factors also include the outer circumstances of life: the particular environment into which a child is born, his culture, and accidents of climate or disease—all of which influence his becoming but are exterior to the process itself.

By opportunistic growth I mean the learning of myriad subsystems that aid our adjustment but never seem to enter the central lattice of life. Such subsystems include automatic biological adaptations, partially reflex in character (respiration, digestion, and the like), as well as many of our tribal conformities (e.g., the wearing of clothes, or brushing of teeth); likewise many of our skills, including the use of our native language. Unless thwarted by outside interferences, these and many other systems run their course through our lifetime without seriously engaging the various propriate functions we have described. The laws of learning generally accepted today are pertinent, I suspect, chiefly to the acquisition of such segmental and opportunistic systems.[37] These systems provide the subsoil of necessary habits upon which propriate development builds.

Adjustments that are at one time propriate may later sink to the opportunistic level. Thus the acquisition of a skill may at first be attended by a keen feeling of propriate involvement. Who can forget the ecstasy of power he felt when he first drove an automobile? And the young child seems no less ecstatic when he first walks successfully, though at such an early age it is doubtful that the experience of ego-enhancement is more than rudimentary. But walking and driving soon become automatic opportunistic systems and may never again be related to the proprium unless thwarted by outside interference. These segmental systems of personality are normally like the fruits

37. G. W. Allport, "Effect: A Secondary Principle of Learning," *Psychological Review*, 53 (1946), 335–47.

of last year's garden. Having served as the crowning glory at one stage of development, they fall into the subsoil and may enrich the products of the next stage of becoming.

What seems to have happened in the course of human evolution is that as man became less instinctive and more intelligent in his transactions he had to develop a focus— a means of transcending the bewildering complexity of myriad *ad hoc* systems of adjustment. Confronted with too many matters of fact, he was forced to develop a discriminating sense of importance. In the language of William James, something was needed to regulate an enterprise grown too top-heavy to regulate itself. According to James this needed monitor was supplied in the evolution of consciousness. It would, I think, be more in keeping with contemporary thought to say that the needed monitor is found in the propriate functions we have described —not all of which are conscious, though all have the effect of conferring a sense of importance upon some realms of conduct and leaving the remainder as opportunistic systems.

This theory has support in ontogenesis, for the behavior of the young infant seems adequately explained in terms of his impulses interacting with an environment that supplies suitable rewards and punishments. It is in this way that early habits are built. But by the age of three life has already grown too complicated for this single mode of becoming. The issues of life call for sorting and assessment in terms of their relative importance, for planning and orientation, for a reference center. And this need grows more acute with time.

Thus the proprium, which we might define as the individual "quality" of organismic complexity, evolves

64

because the human species and the individual human being have need of it. Propriate activity, once evolved, ordinarily has a different subjective texture from opportunistic or chance happenings. We can almost always distinguish between what "happens" to us and what we ourselves "do."

If this line of reasoning is correct, psychology cannot place exclusive reliance upon random and opportunistic theories of becoming. These theories, let me repeat, are good so far as they go. The past fifty years of psychological work, though centered chiefly upon what I have called opportunism in human behavior, have constituted a necessary epoch in our science. It was probably a good thing to have discarded for a while a concept of self which was too inclusive, undiscriminated, and question-begging. But now the time has come to see whether we cannot supplement this scientific sparseness with a cautious account of oriented becoming that will provide a no less accurate but more adequate scientific frame for a psychology of growth.

§ 15. *Motivation and Tension*

A FEW PAGES back, in our discussion of propriate striving, we encountered a point that is so basic to our argument that we venture to repeat it. We saw that most of the theories of motivation favored today have in common one basic assumption, namely that all behavior tends toward the elimination of the exciting state, toward equilibrium, or as the technical phrase has it, toward *drive re-*

duction. Though terminology varies, these theories hold that all excitability, all striving, all tension have their source in the disturbance of organic equilibrium. The more severe the disturbance the greater is the urgency to reduce tension. We learn ways of detensioning to accord with the minimal expenditure of energy. Having thus achieved a successful reduction of tension, we tend to repeat the same mode of relief under similar circumstances of disequilibrium. Some theories place emphasis upon the negative pole of affect (avoidance of pain and discomfort), some on the positive (the attainment of pleasurable consequences). The instincts, says Freud, all strive toward pleasure. Fundamentally the Freudian and behavioristic models are alike; also all other theories holding quiescence, complacency, or pleasure to be the goals of action.

In many respects this model for human motivation is incontestable. Nothing could be more evident than the fact that our drives (hunger for oxygen, for food, for sexual contact) do represent urgent demands for tension-reduction. And yet the more we reflect on the matter the more our suspicion grows that we are dealing here with only half the problem. While we certainly learn habitual modes of reducing tension, we also come to regard many of our past satisfactions to be as worthless as yesterday's ice cream soda. Though we want stability we also want variety. While we learn dependable modes of reducing tension we also abandon old habits and take risks in searching out new courses of conduct. It is only through risk-taking and variation that growth can occur. But risk-taking and variation are fraught with new and often avoidable tensions, which however we scorn to avoid. Hence the formula that seems appropriate enough for

66

drive reduction seems to break down when motivation is no longer a matter of segmental drives or of opportunistic adjustment but rather partakes of propriate striving.

Returning to the case of the explorer Amundsen whose steady progress toward a long-range goal began when he was fifteen years of age, it does not help to say that he was trying all his life to reduce the tension provoked in him at that age by reading the explorations of Sir John Franklin. Such casuistry would neglect the fact that for decades he fought every temptation to relax, to enjoy immediate gratifications that would impede his major effort; he fought the promptings of fatigue, discouragement, social ridicule. Like a true Faustian man he discovered that salvation comes only to him who ceaselessly bestirs himself in the pursuit of objectives that in the end are not fully attained.

Here seems to be the central characteristic of propriate striving: its goals are, strictly speaking, unattainable. Propriate striving confers unity upon personality, but it is never the unity of fulfillment, of repose, or of reduced tension. The devoted parent never loses concern for his child; the devotee of democracy adopts a lifelong assignment in his human relationships. The scientist, by the very nature of his commitment, creates more and more questions, never fewer. Indeed the measure of our intellectual maturity, one philosopher suggests, is our capacity to feel less and less satisfied with our answers to better and better problems.[38]

Nowhere in this endless developmental lattice do we

38. C. W. Churchman, "Ethics, Ideals and Dissatisfaction," *Ethics, an International Journal of Social, Political and Legal Philosophy, 63* (1952), 64f.

find that equilibrium, reward, complacency, provide the sole key to motivation. Nor does the hedonistic conception of the pursuit of "happiness" help us. Happiness is the glow that attends the integration of the person while pursuing or contemplating the attainment of goals. The state of happiness is not itself a motivating force but a by-product of otherwise motivated activity. Happiness is far too incidental and contingent a thing to be considered a goal in itself.

NB

We are thus driven to the conclusion that motives are of two orders, though in a given instance the orders may fuse. To borrow Maslow's terms, there are *deficit* and *growth* motives.[39] Deficit motives do, in fact, call for the reduction of tension and restoration of equilibrium. Growth motives, on the other hand, maintain tension in the interest of distant and often unattainable goals. As such they distinguish human from animal becoming and adult from infant becoming. By growth motives we refer to the hold that ideals gain upon the process of development. Long-range purposes, subjective values, comprehensive systems of interest are all of this order. As one example of growth motives let us consider the dynamics of conscience.

§ 16. Conscience

CONSCIENCE is a crucial agent in the growth of personality. It is a process that controls transitory impulse and opportunistic adjustment in the interests of long-range aim and consistency with the self-image.

39. A. H. Maslow, *Motivation and Personality*.

The prevailing psychological theory of conscience treats it chiefly as a phenomenon of opportunistic learning. It tells us that we learn conscience as we learn any cultural practice, though in the case of conscience it is punishment rather than reward that seems to be the decisive agent. The argument is simple and, up to a point, convincing. The young child receives punishment when he violates a parental taboo. Commands, admonitions, scoldings accompany the infraction and the punishment. After sufficient repetition of this sequence, the child hears the voice of authority whenever he is tempted, and suffers a modified pain when he transgresses.

In any given instance, of course, the sequence of events is complicated. Take the case of a child eighteen months of age. In it we see the first vague wrestling with guilt. The toddler I have in mind seized the lid of a sugar bowl on the dining room table. Loud and frightening admonitions of No! No! greeted his act. Alarmed but yet clearly dominated by the forbidden impulse, the child ran with his booty to the far corner of the room, closed his eyes and held the lid in front of his face, thus seeing no evil and protecting himself in ostrich fashion from the wrath to come. The parents retrieved the property, slapped the child's hands, and induced a tantrum. When the tantrum subsided, the child looked wistfully at the offended mother, clearly bidding for reacceptance. The impulsive act followed by frustration, pain, and anger seemed to awaken affiliative need. We can be sure that if harsh looks and continued scolding are now applied the child will become inconsolable, and the punishment will be almost too harsh for him to bear. But even at best the experience is traumatic, and cannot help but have an effect on future situations of a similar nature. We can predict that the child's next assault on the sugar bowl will probably be accompanied by rudimentary feelings of guilt.

But at eighteen months the child does not yet have an integrated system of conscience. There is rather a congeries of emotional states: the impulse, the fright, the retreat and hiding, the frustration, anger, grief, each having its specific stimulus and specific terminating condition. While the child suffers during this sequence, he does not comprehend what is going on; nor does he refer any portion of the experience to the self-image that develops only later.

Turning to the three-year-old we see more clearly the role of parental identification in the struggle to internalize the voice of conscience. I am indebted for this example to my colleague, Henry A. Murray. A three-year-old boy awoke at six in the morning and started his noisy play. The father, sleepy-eyed, went to the boy's room and sternly commanded him, "Get back into bed and don't you dare get up until seven o'clock." The boy obeyed. For a few minutes all was quiet, but soon there were strange sounds that led the father again to look into the room. The boy was in bed as ordered; but putting an arm over the edge, he jerked it back in, saying, "Get back in there." Next a leg protruded, only to be roughly retracted with the warning, "You heard what I told you." Finally the boy rolled to the very edge of the bed and then roughly rolled back, sternly warning himself, "Not until seven o'clock!" We could not wish for a clearer instance of interiorizing the father's role as a means to self-control and socialized becoming.

At this stage the external voice of authority is in the

process of becoming the internal, or propriate, voice of authority. The parents' task is to enlist the voice in behalf of virtue, as the parents themselves conceive virtue.

To illustrate the prevailing theory at a somewhat later age, let us say the parents take their son into the woods on a family picnic. Under their watchful eyes he picks up the litter after lunch and disposes of it. Perhaps a firm warning on a printed sign, or the sight of a passing constable, may also act as a monitor of neatness. Here still the moral backbone is on the outside.

After a few repetitions of this experience we discover that neither a parent, a sign, nor a constable is needed. The young citizen is socialized. He is mindful of the welfare of those who will follow him at the picnic spot. What now has happened? Is he, as current theory holds, his own policeman and parent, waiting to punish himself for infractions of the tribal code? The theory, we note, states that he abstains from wrongdoing because he fears his own self-punishment. The voice of conscience is the interiorized voice of the herd.

While applicable to the early stages of the growth of conscience, this theory is not convincing for later stages. For one thing, it is not often the violation of tribal taboos or of parental prohibitions that makes us as adults feel most guilty. We now have our private codes of virtue and sin; and what we feel guilty about may have little relation to the habits of obedience we once learned. If conscience were merely a matter of self-punishment for breaking an established habit taught with authority, then we could not account for the fact that we do often discard codes imposed by parents and by culture, and devise codes of our own.

71

We conclude, therefore, that conscience somehow shifts its center from ad hoc habits of obedience to the proprium—that is to say, from opportunistic becoming to oriented becoming. In the course of this shift there occurs an important phenomenological change. The "feel" of conscience in adulthood is seldom tied to the fear of punishment, whether external or self-administered. It is rather an experience of value-related obligation. According to most current psychological theories the essence of conscience is a "must"—a dread of punishment if one commits or omits an action. As we have seen, the early conscience of the child *is* undoubtedly of this order. But when conflicts and impulses come to be referred to the self-image and to propriate striving we find that the sense of obligation is no longer the same as a sense of compulsion; ought is not the same as must. I *must* be careful with matches; I *must* obey traffic regulations; I *mustn't* give way to anger; for disagreeable sanctions will follow if I do so. But I *ought* to write a letter, I *ought* to pick up picnic litter; I *ought* to pursue the good as I conceive it. Whenever I make a self-referred value judgment—as if to say, "This is in keeping with my self-image, that is not"—then I feel a sense of obligation that has no trace of fear in it. To argue that I fear future pangs of conscience is to confuse a possible negative outcome with the wholly positive and immediate sense of obligation, of self-consistency, that is clearly primary.[40]

The point is especially clear when we think of religious conscience. To say that a person performs certain acts and abstains from others because he fears God's punishment

40. Cf. P. A. Bertocci, "A Reinterpretation of Moral Obligation," *Philosophy and Phenomenological Research, 6* (1945), 270–83.

would be to travesty the experience of most religious people, whose consciences have more to do with love than with fear. An inclusive path of life is adopted that requires discipline, charity, reverence, all experienced as lively obligations by a religious person. If we encounter in a personality fear of divine punishment as the sole sanction for right doing, we can be sure we are dealing with a childish conscience, with a case of arrested development.

Conscience in personality is by no means always religiously toned. High moral character is found among the nonreligious. Conscience presupposes only a reflective ability to refer conflicts to the matrix of values that are felt to be one's own. I experience "ought" whenever I pause to relate a choice that lies before me to my ideal self-image. Normally when inappropriate decisions are made, I feel guilt. Guilt is a poignant suffering, seldom reducible in an adult to a fear of, or experience of, punishment. It is rather a sense of violated value, a disgust at falling short of the ideal self-image.

The theory I am here suggesting holds that the must-consciousness precedes the ought-consciousness, but that in the course of transformation three important changes occur. 1. External sanctions give way to internal—a change adequately accounted for by the processes of identification and introjection familiar in Freudian and behavioral theory. 2. Experiences of prohibition, fear, and "must" give way to experiences of preference, self-respect, and "ought." This shift becomes possible in proportion as the self-image and value-systems of the individual develop. 3. Specific habits of obedience give way to generic self-guidance, that is to say, to broad schemata of values that confer direction upon conduct.

73

If early prohibitions and parent identifications were the only source of conscience there would certainly be a fading of conscience in time. It is the generic self-guidance that keeps conscience alive and applicable to new experience. The generic conscience tells us in effect, "If you do this, it will build your style of being; if that, it will tear down your style of being." In proportion as the generic conscience becomes the monitor of growth, emphasis shifts from tribalism to individuality. from opportunistic to oriented becoming. Fear becomes ougnt as propriate development begins to outweigh opportunistic.

Conscience may, like other aspects of personality, be arrested in its development. Plenty of people, adult in years, have not successfully effected these transformations. They suffer from infantile guilt, from unresolved conflicts with early authority figures. But the pathology of conscience does not alter the rules governing its transformations in the normal course of becoming.[41]

41. Some writers (e.g., Bertocci) have argued that since a sense of moral obligation is phenomenologically so different from a collection of childhood "musts" it would be safer to assume that there is an innate capacity to form a sense of obligation independent of the coercions of parent or tribe. My position is somewhat different. While I agree concerning the phenomenological difference, I believe that the observation of children assures us that the must precedes the ought and is a necessary first stage in the process of becoming. For this reason I prefer an emergent to an innate theory of moral obligation.

§ 17. Schemata of Value

THUS IN the moral sphere we may say that becoming depends upon the development of a generic conscience which, in turn, depends upon the possession of long-range goals and an ideal self-image. I may, for example, feel an obligation to give support to the United Nations (it represents a primary "what for" in my life). This broad commitment, to be sure, does not tell me what at any given moment I should do. It is simply a posture of conscience pointing in what for me is the right direction. Similarly, the broad ideal of democratic living, or the principles of Judeo-Christian ethics, or the advancement of one's science, or the best possible education for one's children may serve as guidelines for conduct. Just how such long-range aims are carried in our nervous systems we do not know; but there they are, and they constitute a challenge to the neurophysiology of tomorrow. Parenthetically I venture the opinion that the preoccupation of psychology with behavior that is reactive and punctate rather than with conduct that involves long sequences of time may in large part be due to the infant state of neurophysiology. Elementarism in one science is paralleled by elementarism in the other.

The healthy adult, we know, develops under the influence of value schemata whose fulfillment he regards as desirable even though it may never be completely attained. In agreement with such schemata he selects his perceptions, consults his conscience, inhibits irrelevant or contrary lines of conduct, drops and forms subsystems of

75

habits according as they are dissonant or harmonious with his commitments. In short, in proportion as active schemata for conduct develop they exert a dynamic influence upon specific choices. President Lowell of Harvard was once asked how it was possible for an overworked administrator to make so many detailed decisions day by day. He replied that it was not so difficult as it might seem, for each specific issue fits readily into one of a few dominant categories (schemata) of value. If the administrator is clear in his own mind concerning his value orientations, if he knows his major aims, decisions on specific issues automatically follow.

Few if any of our value-orientations hold the prospect of complete fulfillment. Does any worker for the United Nations, however ardent, really expect a peaceful family of nations in his lifetime? Does the devotee of democracy expect to see his ideal fully realized? The devoutly religious person, however keen his hunger for God, knows that in this world his hunger will not be completely satisfied. Yet all such goals, unattainable as they are, exert a present dynamic effect upon daily conduct, and in so doing direct the course of becoming. How wrong we have been in viewing the process of growth as a reaction to past and present stimuli, neglecting the dynamics of futurity: of orientation, intention, and valuation.

Yet it is necessary to keep a proper balance in this matter. If there has been overemphasis on the opportunistic phases of becoming we should not commit the opposite error and overstress the role of schemata of value. Many individuals, it is plainly evident, lack commitment to ideal goals. For them the future means nothing more than the expectancy of immediate pleasure. One report tells us that 25 per cent of normal college men insist that they have no enthusiasm for any kind of life work.[42] This estimate may not be enlightening, since such expressions of apathy may reflect merely a passing mood. Yet every counsellor knows, as does every therapist, that a persistent problem lies in this state of valuelessness, of anhedonia. One psychotherapist reports that after the turmoil of painful symptoms subsides, many patients still ask the question, "What do I live for?" But these distressing cases, however frequent, merely underscore their departure from the human norm.

Even the best integrated of personalities do not act always consistently with their schemata of value. Irresistible impulse, threads of infantilism, violations of conscience are factors to be reckoned within every life. What is more, the demands of our environment cause us to develop numerous systems of behavior that seem to dwell forever on the periphery of our being. They facilitate our commerce with our world but are never geared into our private lives. We know that we put on an appearance for the occasion, but we know too that such appearance is a masklike expression of our persona and not central to our self-image. Much of our so-called "role behavior" is of this sort. We are all forced to play roles that we regard as alien to us; we know they are not propriate but merely personate.

Yet, in spite of all such conflicts, we develop our personal style of living. Some characteristics of this style lie on the surface and serve to mask our natures. But at the same time, and for the most part, our style proceeds from

42. C. W. Heath, *What People Are: A Study of Normal Young Men* (Cambridge, Harvard University Press, 1945), p. 39.

the proprium outward and cannot help but reveal our schemata of values. A personal style is a way of achieving definiteness and effectiveness in our self-image and in our relationships with other people. It evolves gradually by our adopting a consistent line of procedure and sticking to it.

N.B.

Style is the stamp of individuality impressed upon our adaptive behavior. In our culture and climate we all wear clothes, but our style of dress is individual and revealing. The case is the same with every adaptive act we perform from shaking hands to composing a symphony, from strolling down the street to commanding a regiment.

N.B.

A task for psychology in the future is to find methods for relating style to its fundaments in personality. How much of it reflects tribal folkways, how much is convention and mask, and how, in spite of personateness, do the schemata of value and structured characteristics of personality break through? [43]

§ 18. Anxiety and Culture

THE JUVENILE conscience is fragmentary, consisting of a series of musts as unrelated as brushing one's teeth, avoiding the jam pot, and saying one's prayers—all arbitrary and meaningless prescriptions imposed by the inscrutable will of the parent or other dominant authority.

43. This problem is discussed more fully in G. W. Allport and P. E. Vernon, *Studies in Expressive Movement*, New York, Macmillan, 1933.

78

Early conscience is, as we have shown, an opportunistic conscience. Our later generic conscience, on the other hand, reflects the growing conviction that a state of wholeness is possible even though we continually fight the battle between our impulsive nature and our ideals.

Guilt, doubt, and anxiety are the penalty men pay for having a conscience, whatever its type may be. These states of mind suggest to us the possibility of an ideal course of development wherein conflicts are managed, commitments maintained, and life courageously ordered without recourse to self-deception. Maturity, we feel, means that we should become aware of, and in some way partner to, all the discordant conditions of our own existence.

It is because we are capable of this self-transcendent view that existentialists advise us to accept and participate in the historical, temporal, spatial, biological, psychological, sociological conditions of our lives with such clarity of vision and acceptance of responsibility, and such courage as we can muster.[44]

Just how far the existentialist movement, already well developed in philosophy, literature, and theology, will affect the psychology of personality we cannot yet predict. Already it seems to be a needed blood transfusion. The propositions of existentialism are for the most part stated abstractly or in metaphor. But even so they admonish psychology to strengthen itself in those areas where today it is weak. Existentialism calls for a doctrine of an active intellect, for more emphasis upon propriate functions, in-

44. P. Tillich, *The Courage to Be,* New Haven, Yale University Press, 1953.

cluding self-objectification and oriented becoming. In particular it calls for a wider and fresher view of anxiety, of courage, and of freedom.

It is true that psychology, thanks to Freud, has not neglected the problem of anxiety—at least the type of anxiety aroused by feelings of guilt and fear of punishment. But psychology has little to say about the dread of nonbeing (death) and still less about anxiety over the apparent meaninglessness of existence, which Tillich finds to be the most characteristic anxiety of our times. Because current psychology is one-sided in its treatment of anxiety it falls short also in its view of striving and courage.[45]

Existentialism admits all the evidence that depth psychology can deliver, including every fragment of prose, passion, guilt, and anguish in man's nature; it accepts the fact that opportunism and tribalism cling to our behavior; but it would also give due weight to the dynamic possibilities that lie in self-knowledge, in propriate striving; and would allow for the finite freedom that marks personal choice. Stated in theological terms, the resulting estimate of man's state will include all the factors with which a modern doctrine of regeneration will have to deal.

Broadly speaking, the existentialist view of man devel-

45. There are, of course, exceptions to this statement. In his conception of the "productive personality" Erich Fromm endeavors to develop a formula for adult becoming (*Man for Himself,* New York, Rinehart, 1947). One thinks too of Kurt Goldstein, Carl Rogers, Rollo May, Abraham Maslow, and other clinical and academic theorists. Nor should we overlook the persistent labors of the philosophical school of personalism which for a long time has been demanding that psychological science balance its ledger to give due weight to both the assets and liabilities in human nature.

oped in Europe is more pessimistic than the corresponding American view—a fact that calls our attention to sociocultural influences upon theories of personality. When
life is a hard struggle for existence, and when, as in war-
torn Europe, there appears to be "no exit" (Sartre), then
personalities do in fact grow tense and develop a heavier
sense of duty than of hope. In America, on the contrary,
where the search for a rich, full life suffers fewer impedi-
ments, we expect to find a more open, gregarious, trusting
type of personality. This expectation is reflected in the
prevailing optimism of American psychotherapy which
includes not only neo-psychoanalytic conceptions of a
"productive personality" but also "client-centered therapy" and such flourishing new movements as "pastoral
counseling" and "guidance." Tillich confesses himself as-
tonished by the peculiarly resilient nature of American
courage. "The typical American," he writes, "after he has
lost the foundations of his existence, works for new foundations." [46] "The courage to be as a part in the progress of
the group to which one belongs, of his nation, of all mankind, is expressed in all specifically American philosophies: pragmatism, process philosophy, the ethics of
growth, progressive education, crusading democracy." [47]
Tillich might well have added, in American forms of psychotherapy and guidance as well.

Obviously a man's culture is one of the sets of circumstances from which he draws his style of life. It is never
correct, however, to say that personality is *merely* the
"subjective side of culture." This view is tempting to
anthropologists and sociologists whose attention is pre-

46. *The Courage to Be,* p. 108.
47. *Ibid.,* p. 109.

occupied with the sociocultural conditions of becoming. It is tempting likewise to psychologists who are devoted to the reaction hypothesis; for they see personality as guided chiefly by stimuli, by external instigation, by environmental pressure, by the parent-image. Cultural theories of personality, like other reactive theories, are Lockean rather than Leibnitzian views of human nature. Modern instances are seen in the popular doctrines of "modal personality," "basic personality," "class-linked behavior," and "role theory."

That the cultural approach yields valuable facts we cannot possibly deny, for culture is indeed a major condition in becoming. Yet personal integration is always the more basic fact. While we accept certain cultural values as propriate, as important for our own course of becoming, it is equally true that we are all rebels, deviants, and individualists. Some elements in our culture we reject altogether; many we adopt as mere opportunistic habits, and even those elements that we genuinely *appropriate* we refashion to fit our own personal style of life. Culture is a condition of becoming but is not itself the full stencil.

∫ 19. Freedom

WHEN WE say that we select from the available elements of culture, or that we act in accordance with our conscience, or that we refer our decisions to our schemata of values, we are skirting the problem of freedom. No other issue causes such consternation for the scientific psychologist. One may look through a hundred successive

American books in psychology and find no mention of "will" or "freedom." It is customary for the psychologist, as for other scientists, to proceed within the framework of strict determinism, and to build barriers between himself and common sense lest common sense infect psychology with its belief in freedom. For the same reason barriers are erected against theology. But to our discomfort recent events have raised the issue all over again. Existentialism insists on freedom; much of the psychotherapy now in vogue presupposes it; psychology's new concern with values is at bottom a concern with choices, and therefore revives the problem of freedom. Up to now the tug of war between free will and determinism has been marked by naïveté. Just as we have learned with some success to transcend the monolithic oppositions between mind and body, nature and nurture, we should strive for better perspective in our view of freedom and determinism. The following considerations may help.

1. In the first place, it is essential that we distinguish the viewpoint of the scientist from that of the acting person. The superior wisdom of the scientist may unfortunately blind him to the process of growth that is actually taking place. The scientist's frame of reference is like the frame of an omniscient being: to him all things have time, place, and determined orbits. But this frame is definitely not the frame of the acting person. The situation is much like that of the watcher from the hilltop who sees a single oarsman on the river below. From his vantage point the watcher notes that around the bend of the river, unknown as yet to the oarsman, there are dangerous rapids. What is present to the watcher's eye still lies in the future for the oarsman. The superior being predicts that soon the boat-

83

man will be portaging his skiff—a fact now wholly un-known to the boatman who is unfamiliar with the river's course. He will confront the obstacle when it comes, de-cide on his course of action, and surmount the difficulty. In short, the actor is unable to view his deeds in a large space-time matrix as does an all-wise God, or the less wise demigods of science. From his point of view he is working within a frame of choice, not of destiny. As psychologists we ought to know, and do know, that the way a man de-fines his situation constitutes for him its reality. Choice for him is a paramount fact; how matters appear to the watcher on the hill is irrelevant. It is because existential-ism takes always the acting person's point of view that it insists so strongly upon the attribute of freedom in man's nature.

2. Even when we take the view of the scientist we note that certain conditions make for *relatively* more or less freedom for the individual. One of the conditions we are most sure of is self-insight. A therapist of even the most deterministic persuasion assumes that a patient who achieves a high degree of self-objectification, who sees his personal equation clearly written out, is at last in a posi-tion to weigh his inclinations, comprehend his limita-tions, and follow with some success a self-chosen course of action. If this were not so every system of therapy would operate on false pretense. Psychotherapy gives hope that a corrected self-image, a more rational assessment of one's behavior, will reduce compulsions, induce order, and free channels of development to accord with chosen aims. Hence even a scientific psychology concedes that self-knowledge may lead to a relative freedom.

3. Similarly, relative freedom, we know, depends upon

84

the individual's possession of multiple possibilities for behavior. To state the point paradoxically, a person who
harbors many determining tendencies in his neuropsychic system is freer than a person who harbors few. Thus a
person having only one skill, knowing only one solution,
has only one degree of freedom. On the other hand, a person widely experienced and knowing many courses of
conduct has many more degrees of freedom. It is in this
sense that the broadly educated man is freer than the man
narrowly trained. Today we are witnessing the frightening things that political leaders with one-channeled minds
can do. What alarms us is their simplicist view of social
and political reality. They know only one solution; and
this solution is totalitarian and spurious. Their lack of
tolerance and fear of dissent reflect their own lack of freedom. One-channeled minds can never comprehend that
truth may have many channels. *Cf. Theologians at S. C. C.*

4. Finally, psychology knows that there is relatively
greater freedom in certain modes of choosing than in
others. Man's effort is not particularly effective when he
tries to meet an impulse head on, by cracking his knuckles
and gritting his teeth. Centering attention upon an impulse often brings with it a strong desire to perform the
impulsive act. "The evil I would not, that I do." This law
of "reversed effort" is familiar to us all.[48] And at this level
freedom often seems to be a cruel illusion.

But when I stop cracking my knuckles and become mo-
mentarily reflective, asking myself whether "on the
whole" this is the course of action I want to take, the picture is changed. The very act of asking "on the whole"

48. Cf. William Brown, *Science and Personality* (New Haven,
Yale University Press, 1929), pp. 150–2.

brings with it a lessened strain and opens new pathways of decision. This moment of reflection serves to set into activity the larger systems of propriate striving, and their activation may blot out or absorb incompatible segmental systems and impulses, leaving the individual free to be himself.[49]

The psychologist knows that most of the specific acts we perform ordinarily proceed in accordance with superordinate systems of motivation. If the superordinate system involves, let us say, a loyalty, then the individual, by calling the system to mind, automatically gives it precedence. Under its dominance decisions follow. The weakness of the habit theory lies in assuming that all acts, by the principles of repetition and reward, are theoretically of equal importance in building the structure of personality. Habits appear and disappear not only in conformity with the principles of frequency and reward but also as subsidiary events in relation to a central or propriate structure. William James hastened to repair his doctrine of habits by affirming that the one ultimate act of freedom

49. The point at issue here is of considerable theoretical importance. According to psychoanalytic conceptions the defeated impulse is thought to be repressed, and to continue to plague the individual from the limbo of the unconscious. I am suggesting that under certain circumstances—especially when the comprehensive propriate motive holds sway—the incompatible impulses are not normally repressed; they simply evaporate. Freud himself made a similar observation, though he did not follow through its theoretical implications. In a too seldom quoted passage he writes that he has become "mindful of the distinction between the mere *repression* and the true *disappearance* of an old desire or impulse." [My italics.] S. Freud, *The Problem of Anxiety* (New York, Norton, 1927), pp. 82 f.

at man's disposal is his ability "to keep the selected idea uppermost," by which he meant that when we call upon our self-image we automatically reappraise, inhibit, steer, or activate subordinate courses of conduct. Higher-level systems determine the "go" of the lower, and it is for this reason that man is able to keep as closely as he does to his own major systems of value.

It sometimes happens that the very center of organization of a personality shifts suddenly and apparently without warning. Some impetus, coming perhaps from a bereavement, an illness, or a religious conversion, even from a teacher or book, may lead to a reorientation. In such cases of traumatic recentering it is undoubtedly true that the person had latent within him all of the capacities and sentiments that suddenly rise from a subordinate to a superordinate position in his being. What he had once learned mechanically or incidentally may suddenly acquire heat and liveliness and motor power. What once seemed to him cold, "out there," "not mine" may change places and become hot and vital, "in here," "mine."

I mention this phenomenon of saltatory becoming, not because it is frequent or typical but because it illustrates the complexity and lability of the organizational process. Becoming is not a mere matter of forging links to a chain. It sometimes involves the shifting of dominance from segmental systems to comprehensive systems, or from one comprehensive system to another. Just why or how such shifts occur we cannot say. When they are better understood we can align them with our discussions of determinism and freedom.

These considerations fall short of solving the problem of freedom. They urge us, however, to forego naïve solutions. That there are upper limits to the possibilities of growth in each life no one can deny. But it seems likely that these limits are movable by virtue of the capacities for reflection, for self-objectification, and to a degree by breadth of education, and by the effort an individual may put forth. From the ethical and theological points of view the stretching toward this limit, whatever it is, is as much of a triumph for a life of slight potential as for a life whose potentials are great.

§ 20. Structure of Personality

IN PSYCHOLOGY the problem of becoming is inter-twined with the problem of structure; for process leads to product. In infancy, to be sure, structure is merely rudimentary, composed only of such "dispositions" as may exist (section 6). But as structure takes form it has a decisive influence upon further growth. We predict a friend's behavior because we think we understand his structure. A notable development in recent psychology is the discovery that this structure likewise helps to fashion daily perceptions in ways hitherto unsuspected.[50]

Psychologists handle structure in diverse ways. Every kind of component unit that could be proposed is actually favored by one or more writers as the building blocks of structure. Some talk in terms of needs, sentiments, or vectors; some in terms of traits, attitudes, or values; others

50. H. A. Witkin *et al.*, *Personality through Perception*, New York, Harper, 1954.

prefer habits. We have faculties and factors. One writer proposes units of three orders: motives, schemata, and traits.[51] A few psychologists are content with looser conceptions, such as tendency, trend, or disposition.

For present purposes let us use the venerable Greek term *characteristic* to denote any distinctive mark or engraving of personality. Characteristics can be of many orders, ranging from peripheral mannerisms and opportunistic habits to the most central value-orientations of a life. Since we are interested at the moment in the influence of high-level structure upon subsequent growth, we call attention especially to those characteristics that unite biological vitality with a network of meanings. To adapt a term from medieval philosophy, characteristics of this type represent the person's "intentionality." Intentions, as I shall use the term, are complex propriate characteristics of personality.

Intentional characteristics represent above all else the individual's primary modes of addressing himself to the future. As such they select stimuli, guide inhibitions and choices, and have much to do with the process of adult becoming. Relatively few theories of personality recognize the pre-emptive importance of intentional characteristics. While recent empirical investigations have abundantly proved that personal values do in fact steer and select perceptions, judgments, and adjustments, there is still inadequate recognition of the theoretical significance of this discovery. To be sure, some years ago the German school of *Verstehendepsychologie* insisted that the major characteristic of any personality is the individual's philos-

51. D. C. McClelland, *Personality*, New York, Sloane, 1951.

ophy of life, that is to say, his value-system, his *Lebens-verfassung*.[52] The point has recently been stated more crisply by Professor Paul Weiss who rightly maintains that "We know our fellows because we know the kind of future they are bringing about." [53]

It is encouraging to note that experimentalists are now starting to work on the dynamics of value-schemata. Many of the recent studies of perceptual and cognitive processes are enlightening. Even industrial psychology is learning that long-range intentions guide learning, productivity, and the satisfaction of the worker on the job. A vocational counselor has told me that the most revealing question he asks in his interviews is "Where do you want to be five years from now?" The significance of this question is identical with Professor Weiss's slightly more abstract phrasing, "What kind of a future are you bringing about?" Thus from various sources and from diverse points of view we are commencing to understand that value-schemata are decisive factors in becoming.

Philosophically speaking, values are the termini of our intentions. We never fully achieve them. Some writers make much of this fact. Jung, for example, defines personality in terms of the ideal state of integration toward which the individual is tending. Personality is not what one has, but rather the projected outcome of his growth. Similarly, Spranger views the character of an individual

52. W. Dilthey, "Ideen uber eine beschreibende und zergliedernde Psychologie; Beiträge zum Studium der Individualität," *Gesammelte Schriften*, 5, 1895. Also E. Spranger, *Types of Men*. Halle, Max Niemeyer Verlag, trans. 1928.

53. P. Weiss, *Man's Freedom* (New Haven, Yale University Press, 1950), p. 170.

in terms of his approximation to an ideal type (an ultimately self-consistent value system). It is the orientation
that is important. From this point of view we may modify
slightly our contention that complex levels of structure
influence becoming. More precisely stated, it is the un-
finished structure that has this dynamic power. A finished
structure is static; but a growing structure, tending
toward a given direction of closure, has the capacity to
subsidiate and guide conduct in conformity with its movement.

The question arises: How many major characteristics,
intentional or otherwise, may we expect a personality to
have? In writing on the *Thought and Character of
William James,* Ralph Barton Perry states that in order
to understand this brilliant and humane personality it is
necessary to comprehend four morbid and four benign
characteristics.[54] At first it seems outrageous to us that so
subtle and complex a person can be compressed into a
simple mold. We should be enraged if a biographer tried
such highhanded surgery upon us.

Yet, on second thought, may we not here be approaching an important discovery? For all the baffling complexity of growth, is it not true that at the highest levels of integration the structure of a personality clarifies? When
the many threads are assembled we perceive that they are

54. 2 vols. Boston, Little, Brown, 1936. "An inventory of James's
pathological traits would embrace, then, tendencies to hypochon-
dria and hallucinatory experience, abnormally frequent and intense oscillations of mood, and an almost morbid alogism, or an-
tipathy to the mode of thinking which employs definitions, symbols,
and trains of inference. . . . Turning to James's benign traits, I
find four that are peculiarly pervasive: sensibility, vivacity, hu-
manity, and sociability." (2, 681f.)

woven into cables. The cables serve the function of bind-
ing the individual to the world in terms of major meanings. While the science of psychodiagnosis has not yet
dealt extensively with this problem, I suggest that the
musical metaphor of *Leitmotiven* may be a helpful guide.
In his *Experiment in Autobiography*, H. G. Wells tells us
that two dominant themes cover almost all of his life
history. These, he says, are first his interest in the achievement of an ordered world society; and second, sex.[55] We
may suspect that this autodiagnosis is somewhat simpli-
fied, but the point is there and should be explored by psychologists. A leading motif, as in the case of Wells's interest in one world, may be highly socialized and may
represent value-schemata of the type that accompany an
extended self and a generic conscience. Or it may on occasion be a neurotic formation, an unresolved parent complex, or one of many forms of narcissism. But our essential
hypothesis remains unchanged: the forces of organization
are so strong that in any given case a few leading characteristics do in fact depict the course of growth.

NB To summarize: the most comprehensive units in personality are broad intentional dispositions, future-
pointed. These characteristics are unique for each person,
and tend to attract, guide, inhibit the more elementary
units to accord with the major intentions themselves.
This proposition is valid in spite of the large amount of
unordered, impulsive, and conflictful behavior in every
life. Finally, these cardinal characteristics are not infinite
in number but for any given life in adult years are relatively few and ascertainable. This fact should encourage

55. New York, Macmillan, 1934, pp. 12 and 348.

psychodiagnosticians to seek methods more appropriate than some they now employ.

§ 21. The Religious Sentiment

IF WE ask what psychology has contributed to our understanding of the religious nature of man, the answer is "Less than we might wish." We can explain and to some extent justify this backwardness by pleading the inherent difficulties in working out a scientific psychology of the more complex stages of growth. The religious sentiment, we are now in a position to understand, has attachments to the most elusive facets of becoming, including propriate striving, generic conscience, and intentionality.

We may, to be sure, point to three modest lines of scientific advance in the present century. 1. In his examination of the varieties of religious experience, William James provided us with an excellent typology which, in spite of its looseness, is difficult to improve upon. 2. Modern methods of questionnaires and polling give us reliable, if superficial, data on the extent of religious beliefs and opinions. 3. Depth psychology has made us aware of the role of unconscious processes, particularly of those that impede normal integrative growth. One of the chief merits of depth psychology is its wholesome warning against projecting one's own sentiments into scientific discussions. The danger of projection is, of course, especially acute in discussions of religion where ambiguities of meaning are so prevalent.

93

If, however, our outline of the process of becoming has validity, certain consequences for the psychological understanding of religion follow. First of all, our analysis warns us against the trivial view that holds adult religion to be merely a repetition of the experiences of the child. Although a child may sometimes extend the image of his earthly father to a divine Father, it is a nonsequitur to say that all religious adults do the same. True, some adults may never outgrow their tendency to cling to a partisan deity who, like an overindulgent father, responds always to special pleading. Yet the healthy person in possession of normal intelligence, insight, and emotional maturity knows that he cannot solve life's problem by wishful thinking or cure his own partialness by fictionizing. To cure his partialness he must find something more convincing than partialness itself. Hence the developed personality will not fabricate his religion out of some emotional fragment but will seek a theory of Being in which all fragments are meaningfully ordered.

The developed religious sentiment, therefore, cannot be known in terms of its many empirical origins. It is not a mere matter of dependency or of reliving the family or cultural configuration: nor is it simply a prophylaxis against fear; nor is it an exclusively rational system of belief. Any single formula by itself is too partial. The developed religious sentiment is the synthesis of these and many other factors, all of which form a comprehensive attitude whose function it is to relate the individual meaningfully to the whole of Being.

To feel oneself meaningfully linked to the whole of Being is not possible before puberty. This fact helps to explain the one-sided emphasis we encounter in many

94

psychological discussions of religion. Becoming has been much more thoroughly studied for the years preceding puberty than for adolescent and adult years. It is, therefore, understandable that the factors influencing the religion of childhood should loom large in our present view: familism, dependence, authority, wishful thinking, and magical practice.

Since, however, the process of becoming continues throughout life, we rightly expect to find the fully developed sentiment only in the adult reaches of personality. The adult mind, provided that it is still growing, stretches its rational capacities as far as it can with the logic of induction, deduction, and a weighing of probabilities. While the intellect continues to exert itself, the individual finds that he needs to build aspiring defenses against the intellect's almost certain failure. He learns that to surmount the difficulties of a truculent world he needs also faith and love. Thus religion, engaging as it does reason, faith, and love, becomes for him morally true. Most religious people claim that it is also metaphysically true because they feel that outer revelation and mystical experience have brought them supernatural assurance. Thus the warrant for certitude comes from the total orientation that the person attains in his quest for a comprehensive belief-system capable of relating him to existence as a whole.

Psychologically speaking, we should point to the close analogy that exists between a religious orientation and all other high-level schemata that influence the course of becoming. Every man, whether he is religiously inclined or not, has his own ultimate presuppositions. He finds he cannot live his life without them, and for him they are

95

true. Such presuppositions, whether they be called ideologies, philosophies, notions, or merely hunches about life, exert creative pressure upon all conduct that is subsidiary to them (which is to say, upon nearly *all* of a man's conduct).

The error of the psychoanalytic theory of religion—to state the error in its own terminology—lies in locating religious belief exclusively in the defensive functions of the ego rather than in the core and center and substance of the developing ego itself. While religion certainly fortifies the individual against the inroads of anxiety, doubt, and despair, it also provides the forward intention that enables him at each stage of his becoming to relate himself meaningfully to the totality of Being.

From this line of reasoning we might expect most adults to be religious people, as in fact they are. Yet there is endless diversity among them in the degree to which religion plays a part in their lives, and in the forms and relative maturity of their religious outlook.[56] It could not be otherwise, for religious becoming is influenced by our temperament and training, and is subject to arrest as well as growth. Some of the arresting forces leave the individual with an infantile form of religious belief, self-serving and superstitious. Neurotic insecurities may demand an immediate and compulsive ritual of reassurance. Sometimes the extreme rigidity of training in the home or church presents only a partial criterion for testing truth, with the result that the child may either grow fiercely partisan and intolerant or else at a later age react against his training and embrace a negative attitude of unbelief.

56. Cf. G. W. Allport, *The Individual and His Religion,* New York, Macmillan, 1950.

There are many conditions that make for arrested development.

All phases of becoming are subject to arrest. Psychopathy may be regarded as an arrest in self-extension, so that no sense of moral obligation evolves. Exhibitionism and other perversions are arrests in genital development; narcissism an arrest in the growth of the self-image. Infantilism in religion results in an arrest due to the immediate needs for comfort and security or self-esteem. Unbelief, while it may be the product of mature reflection, may also be a reaction against parental or tribal authority, or may be due to a one-sided intellectual development that rules out other areas of normal curiosity.[57] We find many personalities who deal zealously and effectively with all phases of becoming except the final task of relating themselves meaningfully to creation. For some reason their curiosity stops at this point.

Others, however, devote themselves wholly to this task. Their religious aspiration is their cardinal characteristic. For them the religious form of propriate striving alone seems worth while. It provides them with a synthesis of all that lies within experience and all that lies beyond. It monitors the growing edge of personality. Such individuals exercise their capacity for self-objectification, viewing with detachment their reason and their unreason, seeing the limitations of both. They hold in perspective both their self-image and ideal self-image, thus providing themselves with a criterion for conscience. They discriminate between their propriate striving and their opportunistic adjustments, thus distinguishing matters of import-

57. Cf. H. C. Rümke, *The Psychology of Unbelief*, trans. from the Dutch, London, Rockliff, 1953.

ance from mere matters of fact. They weigh probabilities in the theological realm, and ultimately affirm a view of life that seems to leave the least possible remainder. Intricate as the process is, it seems to be the way in which mature personalities adopt and validate the religious premise of their course of becoming.

As a science, psychology can neither prove nor disprove religion's claims to truth. It can, however, help explain why these claims are so many and so diverse. They represent the final meanings achieved by unique personalities in diverse lands and times. Organized religious sects reflect comparable sets of meanings within which the unique meanings achieved by individuals may cluster for purposes of communication and common worship.

Psychology can also illuminate the field of religion by following the course of becoming to its ultimate frontiers of growth. It can study man as a representative of his species, as a creature of many opportunistic adjustments, and as a product of tribal molding. But it can study him as well as a self-assertive, self-critical, and self-improving individual whose passion for integrity and for a meaningful relation to the whole of Being is his most distinctive capacity. By devoting itself to the entire course of becoming—leaving out no shred of evidence and no level of development—psychology can add progressively to man's self-knowledge. And as man increases in self-knowledge he will be better able to bind himself wholesomely and wisely to the process of creation.

The final truths of religion are unknown, but a psychology that impedes understanding of the religious potentialities of man scarcely deserves to be called a logos of the human psyche at all.

98

§ 22. *Epilogue: Psychology and Democracy*

I HAVE written this essay because I feel that modern psychology is in a dilemma. Broadly speaking, it has trimmed down the image of man that gave birth to the democratic dream. Insofar as the scaling down has accorded with reality it is all to the good, for it is not wholesome to live by illusion. Eighteenth-century conceptions of man, from which much of the early enthusiasm for democracy originated, stood in need of correction. Modern psychology points to the marshland of unreason in human nature whose seepage clouds man's judgment at the ballot box and stultifies his outlook. To a marked degree culture, class membership, and their respective prejudices mold both conscience and conduct. Early fixations in character often leave infantile traces that bind the mind in such a way that democratic relationships in adult life are impossible. Infantile complexes of guilt may defeat the development of a generic conscience whose code is one of respect for all persons.

All this is true—yet the question is whether such "realism" is not as one-sided as the rationalistic theory of human nature upon which democracy was founded. May it not be that partial methods and oversimplified models are adapted only to the discovery of the cruder mechanical determinants of personality? Animal analogies, pathologies, emphasis upon external rather than internal forces are understandable in the early stages of scientific psychology. It will take time to develop methods and theories suited to the less accessible regions of personality

99

reflected in its structuring, generic conscience, and propriate schemata.

Up to now the "behavioral sciences," including psychology, have not provided us with a picture of man capable of creating or living in a democracy. These sciences in large part have imitated the billiard ball model of physics, now of course outmoded. They have delivered into our hands a psychology of an "empty organism," pushed by drives and molded by environmental circumstance. What is small and partial, what is external and mechanical, what is early, what is peripheral and opportunistic—have received the chief attention of psychological system builders. But the theory of democracy requires also that man possess a measure of rationality, a portion of freedom, a generic conscience, propriate ideals, and unique value. We cannot defend the ballot box or liberal education, nor advocate free discussion and democratic institutions, unless man has the potential capacity to profit therefrom. In *The Measure of Man,* Joseph Wood Krutch points out how logically the ideals of totalitarian dictatorships follow from the premises of "today's thinking" in mental and social science. He fears that democracy is being silently sabotaged by the very scientists who have benefited most from its faith in freedom of inquiry.

Curiously enough, many of the ardent adherents to the "empty organism" theory of human nature are among the most zealous fighters for democracy. No paradox is more striking than that of the scientist who as citizen makes one set of psychological assumptions and in his laboratory and writings makes opposite assumptions respecting the nature of man.

Given time it seems probable that psychology will

ripen in the direction of democracy's basic assumptions. Some of the considerations we have reviewed indicate that the evolution is well under way. The emerging figure of man appears endowed with a sufficient margin of reason, autonomy, and choice to profit from living in a free society. The portrait, however, does not discard the darker portion of truth discovered by the youthful psychology of the recent past. This truth stands, and it will ever remain the duty of psychology to correct idealistic exuberance.

But since psychology is a nonnormative discipline it is unable by itself to provide the stencil of values by which to assess the course of becoming. Democracy is one such value-stencil offered to test growth both in the individual and in human society. What psychology can do is to discover whether the democratic ideal is viable. According to some of the partial truths now established and widely accepted the answer seems negative. But this answer is far from final. As we become more adept in dealing with the whole fabric of personality we discover potentialities of greater promise. Soon, we venture to predict, psychology will offer an image of man more in accord with the democratic ideals by which psychologists as individuals do in fact live.

Index

103

THE YALE PAPERBOUNDS